The gift of grace

The gift of grace

Roman Catholic teaching in the light of the Bible

T. Vanhuysse

 EVANGELICAL PRESS

EVANGELICAL PRESS
12 Wooler Street, Darlington, Co. Durham, DL1 1RQ, England

© Evangelical Press 1992
First English edition 1992

First published in French under the title *L'Assurance du Salut* by Stichting Tot Bevordering Van De Evangelieverkondiging in Belgie

British Library Cataloguing in Publication Data available

ISBN 0 85234 298 5

Printed and bound in Great Britain by Bath Press, Avon

Contents

Introduction

Many Christians wonder from time to time, 'What exactly is an indulgence? How does a Roman Catholic come to earn indulgences?' I have tried for a long time to look at this topic from all angles and I have come to the conclusion that the question is so important that I have devoted this work to answering it. But, we may ask, when time is at such a premium, is it really worthwhile spending so much of it discussing a question of this nature? However, I decided that this enquiry was necessary for the following reason: the practice of indulgences is typical of the very essence of Roman Catholicism, namely, the role of good works, produced by the power of grace.

Quite apart from biblical considerations, this idea seems to be a contradiction in terms, but this is not the case in Roman Catholic ideology. Professor Van de Pol writes in *The Christian Dilemma* (1948): 'Good works do not provide any basis for personal pride, for we owe our good works to the work of grace effected by the Holy Spirit.' We could almost speak in terms of 'by faith alone, by Catholic grace alone'. Here too we come to the crux of the Roman Catholic doctrine of justification, that is, the meritorious nature of good works.

I am convinced that in order to be able to understand the Catholic doctrine of justification it is essential to have an understanding of their doctrine of grace. This also explains the lack of assurance of salvation and the inner insecurity which characterize the sincere Catholic believer.

This passionate longing for a sense of certainty and peace

of mind in matters of faith was expressed in its most intense form in the battle fought by Luther. Luther's words about the 'righteousness of God' therefore seem a particularly apt introduction to our present study.

'For in it the righteousness of God is revealed from faith to faith; as it is written, "The just shall live by faith"' (Rom. 1:17).

Luther writes, about this verse, 'I used to hate this expression, the "righteousness of God", for common usage and the way it is normally used by all the learned doctors had taught me to understand it in a philosophical sense. I understood it to mean the righteousness which they call formal or active, according to which God is just and which causes him to punish sinners and those who are guilty. Despite the blameless nature of my life as a monk, I felt that I was a sinner before God; my conscience was extremely troubled and I had no certainty that God was appeased by my attempts to satisfy him. So I had no love for this righteous and vengeful God. I hated him, and if I did not actually go as far as to blaspheme him in secret, I was certainly filled with indignation and murmured violently against him, saying, "Isn't it enough that he condemns us to eternal death because of the sin of our fathers and that he makes us undergo all the severity of his law? Must he also add to our torment by the gospel and even in that tell us of his righteousness and his wrath? My conscience was so violently wrought upon that I was beside myself and I returned again and again to the study of this passage of St Paul in a passionate desire to know what St Paul actually meant.

'At last, God took pity on me. While I was meditating day and night and examining the connection between these words, "The righteousness of God is revealed in the gospel; as it is written, 'The just shall live by faith,'" I began to understand that in this passage the righteousness of God means the righteousness which God gives and by which the just lives, if he has faith. The meaning of the sentence must therefore be as follows: the gospel reveals to us the righteousness of God, but it is the "passive righteousness", by which God in his mercy justifies us through faith, as it is written: "The just shall live by faith." Immediately I felt as if I were born anew, and I seemed to have entered through wide-open gates into paradise itself. From then on the whole of Scripture appeared to me in a different light. I went over the various texts as they sprang to memory and noted other terms which had to be explained in a similar way, such as "the work of God", that is, the work which God accomplishes in us, "the power of God", by which he gives us strength, the "wisdom", by which he makes us wise, the "salvation" and the "glory" of God.

'Just as I had previously hated this term, the "righteousness of God", so now I loved and cherished this word which was so full of sweetness. And that was how this passage of St Paul became for me the gateway into Paradise. Afterwards I read Augustine on *The Spirit and the Letter*, where I was amazed to discover that he interprets "the righteousness of God" in a very similar way; in other words, he understands it to mean the righteousness with which God clothes us when he justifies us. And although Augustine still expresses himself imperfectly and does not explain clearly all about imputation or righteousness, I had the joy of finding that he taught that we should understand the righteousness of God to be that by which we are justified.'[1]

When Luther entered the convent of Erfurt in 1505, it was with the intention of meeting a God of grace. Dr W. Van't Spijker writes in his book, *Luther, the Promise and the Experience,* 'And he should certainly have found him there, if there had been any truth in the great monastic system, with its aspirations after fulness, and its quest for peace of mind. If it had been true that we must do what we can and that this is indeed a way to salvation, then Luther should have found this way, and the peace of mind that went with it. In fact he found doubt, temptations, despair, distress and a permanent lack of assurance which made him afraid both to live or to die.

'But in the midst of all that, the Holy Spirit revealed Holy Scripture to him... And Scripture revealed to him a merciful

God, who in Christ imputes to us righteousness, a righteousness which is obtained by faith alone.

'Luther's discovery was nothing less than a discovery of the gospel itself, given to him from above as he listened to, and learned from, Holy Scripture.'

As the light of Scripture is allowed to shine on the Roman doctrine of grace and the practice of indulgences, may it be a warning for us all to keep 'holding fast the faithful word' (Titus 1:9), and at the same time an encouragement to walk as children of light, for the fruit of the Spirit is in all goodness, righteousness and truth (Eph. 5:8-9).

1.
Grace and free will

Anyone reading the conclusions reached by the Council of Orange could be forgiven for thinking that the document before him was an affirmation of the teachings of the apostle Paul. At this council it was clearly laid down as a doctrine of the church that the whole man is corrupted by sin and that faith 'in its beginnings as well as in its development' cannot be attributed to ourselves, but to the grace of God. The freedom of the will is curtailed and Rome even speaks of this being so limited that no one can love God as he should, nor believe in God or do good without the prevenient grace of God's mercy.

The Council of Orange teaches that 'If anyone were to say that by his own natural resources he can conceive of or desire any good thing which leads to eternal life; or that he can believe the preaching of the gospel, which is the means of salvation, without the illumination and inner witness of the Holy Spirit ... then he has gone astray into heretical teaching, without having understood the divine word of the gospel: "Without me, you can do nothing.""[1]

The Council of Trent confirmed this position: 'If anyone shall say, that the divine grace though Jesus Christ is given only unto this, that man may more easily be able to live justly, and to merit eternal life, as if, by free will without grace, he were able [to do] both, though hardly and with difficulty; let him be anathema.

'If anyone shall say, that without the preventing inspiration of the Holy Ghost, and his help, man can believe, hope, love, or be penitent, as he ought, so that the grace of justification may be conferred upon him; let him be anathema.'[2]

But the same Council of Orange which made the
statement quoted above speaks elsewhere of the co-
operation which Christ grants to those who have received
baptism, so that they may attain salvation 'if they will
themselves work to achieve it' (*'si fideliter laborare
voluerint'*).[3]

Surely that sounds like 'co-operation on man's part'? It
would seem to mean that salvation is considered as being
dependent on two factors, namely grace and freedom of
choice. Can we speak of the sovereign grace of God in this
way? I believe that by making such a declaration Rome is
really attacking the essential nature of divine grace, as it
relates to man. For if 'grace' and 'free will' are understood
as Rome portrays them, as independent factors which co-
operate with each other, then human merit is taken into
account, alongside the divine initiative. Rome sees them as
two independent factors which complement each other. But
it becomes very clear that if this is the case man must
therefore be able to work for his salvation by his own efforts.

This idea of personal ability always rears its ugly head
sooner or later! Oh, how hard it is to be willing to depend on
grace alone and nothing else! We are by nature far too proud
to admit that we are totally depraved. One way or another, we
want to keep some part of the credit for ourselves.

But if we attribute even the tiniest part of our salvation to
ourselves, this minimal degree of co-operation on our part
ultimately becomes the decisive factor in determining
whether or not we are saved. The following illustration will
show what I mean.

On the one hand, let's suppose there is a giant
petrochemical company with a whole army of engineers,
drilling equipment and vast capital resources, and on the
other a peasant farmer who owns a small plot of land. Now
as it happens, there is oil beneath his land. The farmer knows
nothing at all about oil; nor does he have the money to exploit
this resource. All that is asked of him is that he append his
signature to a bill of sale already drawn up by the company
lawyer. It may only be an untidy scrawl, but that signature
will decide whether or not any of the oil can be extracted.

Thus the grace of God is stripped of all real meaning and content as long as anything pertaining to human nature is regarded as having any worth, if any degree of human participation is introduced into the redemptive work of God. I shall endeavour to examine this concept at greater depth in the chapter on good works.

The Catholic doctrine of grace amounts to saying that man cannot 'live by grace alone'. Everything in our nature rises up in protest against that assertion. Who would say, on his own initiative, that he was 'dead in trespasses and sins'? (Eph. 2:1). You can imagine the reaction: 'Come off it! I'm not as bad as all that!' How high and mighty man can be! I remember how I fought against accepting the Word of God which showed me very plainly what I was like in my innermost being: incapable of doing good and inclined towards all kinds of evil, cut off from all hope of salvation and doomed to a horrible state of perdition (Eph. 2:12). This Word of God, which is so living and powerful and so sharp that it can pierce deep into our hearts — this Word strips bare all our thoughts and arguments and brings us to discover what we really are: miserable, self-centred creatures, inflated with pride and greedy for honour and praise.

Even Bible-believing Christians are not totally free from these things. How vehemently we rise up in opposition one against the other, seething with inner hostility! Let us all examine ourselves. How easily God's children raise their voices against each other! How much distress that causes in the Body of Christ! Is there not something infinitely sad about these words of the Lord to his people: 'With your mouth you have boasted against me and multiplied your words against me; I heard them'? (Ezek. 35:13).

Anyone who tastes 'the bread of grace' becomes humble and modest. A man cannot in any way contribute to the redemptive work of God! It is only God's sovereign grace which assures man's salvation. 'For the grace of God that brings salvation has appeared to all men' (Titus 2:11). Let us make sure that we understand this: we do not have to serve God so that he should save us. He saves us by grace so that we should serve him.

'Merit on the basis of grace'

The principal concern of the Council of Orange was the relationship between God's sovereign grace and the fact that human free will had been rendered null and void. This relationship was chiefly considered in terms of a balance of power and of actions, but very little is said in the documents about justifying grace, unmerited pardon and the acquittal of the guilty.

That, I think, is the basic problem with the Councils of Orange and Trent: the concept of 'merit on the basis of grace'. Surely that is the fundamental problem with the Roman Catholic Church. It was that very point which brought about the split between Rome and the Reformers. Oh, what a serious mistake the Roman Catholic Church made! And because of that mistake, thousands and thousands have been led astray and lost eternally! Because of that mistake thousands of sincere Christians were persecuted and even sent to the stake. What grief that must cause the Lord, our God!

Is Rome blind to the gospel of grace, then? They continue to reject the idea that man's 'free will' is lost and powerless to act. Rome still teaches that human nature was not irrevocably lost by the Fall, so that man is not deprived of the free exercise of his will. Human nature has indeed been affected and man's free will impaired, but, they say, it is not certain that human nature is entirely corrupt. Consequently Rome can also teach that man, by virtue of his natural nobility of character, is able to remove the obstacles which stand between him and friendship with God. It is this natural nobility which makes possible God's coming as a Redeemer and the establishment of a relationship between God and man. Can Rome not see what an intrusion it is on the part of man to make him a co-worker with God in his plan of salvation?

What does Rome make of Romans 8:19-23? The Bible expressly teaches that the whole creation sighs and groans in suffering and is subject to the bondage of corruption. Oh, the horror of sin! Yet Rome teaches: 'If anyone shall say, that, since Adam's sin, the free will of man is lost and extinguished; or, that it is a thing with a name only, yea, a title without a reality, a figment, in fine, brought into the church by Satan; let him be anathema.'[4]

What about Romans 3, then? Or what about these words of Job chapter 15:

'What is man, that he could be pure?
And he who is born of a woman, that he could be
    righteous?
If God puts no trust in his saints,
And the heavens are not pure in his sight,
How much less man, who is abominable and filthy,
Who drinks iniquity like water!'

(Job 15:14-16).

Oh, yes, the Council of Trent also teaches: 'If anyone does not confess that the first man, Adam, when he had transgressed the commandment of God in paradise, immediately lost the holiness and justice in which he had been constituted; and that he incurred, through the offence of such prevarication, the wrath and indignation of God, and consequently death, which God had previously threatened to him, and, together with death, captivity under the power of him who thenceforth had the empire of death, that is to say, the devil, and that the entire Adam, through that offence of prevarication, was changed as respects the body and soul, for the worse; let him be anathema.'[5]

Rome's 'optimistic view of human nature'

The statement we have just read sounds almost like a Reformed confession of the depravity of human nature. However, it must be said that Rome certainly does not mean that. In saying this, Rome has no intention of confessing the radical depravity of human nature; the contrary proves to be the case, if we look at the many and varied ways in which Rome has understood such expressions as 'grace' and 'justification'.

What comes across in these writings is a much more optimistic view of human nature. Rome acts as the protector of human nature and advocates a kind of 'anthropological optimism'. This also becomes apparent both from a comparison between the different conclusions reached by the Council of Trent, and from Rome's opposition to an over-emphasis of the consequences of original sin.

On this very point, they do not hesitate to part company even with Augustine, whose writings are nevertheless regarded as authoritative in the theology of Rome. Writing in his *Manual of Church History*, Cardinal De Jong wrote on this subject: 'And in his fiery rhetoric, he gives so much emphasis to one aspect of established truth, the need for grace, that he seems to deny the complementary truth of free will. The church has never adopted as its beliefs certain implications of Augustine's teachings on grace: his pessimistic view of human nature, the gloomy and harsh way in which he depicts the omnipotence and justice of God, his explanation of original sin, his doctrine of effective grace, of predestination and the small number of the elect.'

Rome considers that Augustine was guilty of exaggeration when he taught that the whole of human nature is radically corrupted as a result of the sin of Adam and is liable to eternal damnation. They can no longer go along with Augustine when he teaches that, without grace, man is a miserable sinner. He must have lost his sense of proportion and balance!

'On the whole, at the time of the Renaissance, the image of the world was distorted, as a result of the intransigent doctrine of Augustine and, in opposition to the Reformers, the church defended human nature as well as the divine will to save; it did not consider this nature to be eternally lost and deprived of all salvation outside of grace, but rather as wounded and capable of being healed. The optimistic view of original sin became more clearly defined and ... according to Trent the theologians and saints remained optimistic in the way they described original sin.'[6]

Rome is optimistic about human nature. They have even been known to speak of a certain degree of 'sensitivity' towards grace on the part of sinful man, of a natural disposition towards grace: 'It is the natural sensitivity of the human spirit which does not put any obstacle in the way of a more intimate relationship with the Spirit of God, but rather aspires towards being made a child of God as an unhoped for treasure, while at the same time nature and grace co-operate in such a way that grace comes to the aid of nature and nature to the support of grace.'[7]

What a comfort it is to be able to rely on the Word of God, which establishes so clearly that there can be no question of any co-operation between grace and free will!

Augustine

In an article on Augustine, one of the church fathers, Dr. W. Aalders quotes 'the dramatic decline of the Abbey of Port-Royal in France' as an example of the influence exerted by Augustine on the history of the Roman Catholic Church. He writes, 'A number of brilliant books have been published on this subject, the most significant of which are the six-volume work of Sainte-Beuve, *Port Royal,* and A. Gazier's *General History of the Jansenist Movement.* What happened in the time of Louis XIV, in the area around Paris, was in fact a major conflict between the powerful and very influential order of the Jesuits and the spiritual heirs of Augustine. All and sundry rallied round to eradicate from the church every last trace of the spirit of Augustine. They left no stone unturned in order to obtain their objective. They would not rest until they had achieved what they wanted: "Raze it, raze it, to its very foundation!" (Ps. 137:7). They did not leave one stone upon another; no tomb was spared, nor a single monument left intact.'

Where did all this animosity and aggressiveness come from? It was none other than the old controversy which has so often set Christendom ablaze. Cost what it may, man tries to increase his own standing in the face of sovereign grace. Did not Luther speak of the 'poison, injected by the old dragon, which deeply contaminated Adam and his descendants'?

How was that able to provoke a revival of the spirit of Augustine behind the walls of Port-Royal? It all began, not in France, but in Flanders, at the University of Louvain. At the Council of Trent, the Roman church had consigned to damnation Luther's teaching, his doctrine of free and sovereign grace and the appropriation of the latter by faith alone. This was what Augustine had also taught and preached in days gone by and it was this which had naturally made the Bishop of Hippo into something of a problem figure for many Roman Catholics. Following the arrival on the scene of the Reformer, who, it should be noted, belonged to the Augustinian order and often appealed to Augustine in support of his teaching, the authority of the church father came under a fierce attack. It was the Jesuits in particular who, after the Council of Trent, spoke of him with contempt, as of someone who did not know how to control his tongue, someone who was unbalanced, prone to flights of rhetoric, fluctuating wildly from one extreme to another; someone whose influence had been more harmful than helpful to the church.

The result of all this was that serious thinkers made it their business to try harder than ever before to determine exactly what this church father had taught and preached. One such person was the professor at Louvain, Cornelius Jansen, who was later to become Bishop of Ypres. For more than twenty years this scholar quietly undertook a thorough and sustained examination of all Augustine's writings. At the end of it all he published his findings in a thick volume entitled *Augustinus* (1640). In it he showed that Augustine had taught the irresistible nature of grace and that man without grace was incapable of any good. Only the initiative of divine grace could liberate man from the snare of carnal desires. The professor did not realize that he had thrown a lighted torch into the midst of the Catholic Church. He never felt the results of his actions, because the fire only broke out after his death.

This occurred when Jansen's book was read and welcomed with approval and gratitude in the Abbey of Port-Royal, near Paris. The study of this work led to a sudden discovery of the relevance of Augustine's thought, first by all those living in the abbey, and subsequently also by all who maintained close relations with the abbey and were described as the friends of Port-Royal. Among the latter were a number of those who moved in royal circles, artists and writers, men such as Pascal, Corneille and Racine, to name but three. The result was that Jansen's book on Augustine became a topic of conversation throughout the whole of Paris.

The Jesuits, who were positively contemptuous when they spoke of the church father, even dared to claim that in fact the Council of Trent had condemned not only Lutheranism and Calvinism, but also the Augustinian doctrine of grace. They even went as far as to say that Molina, a theologian of the Society of Jesus, had proved how detrimental Augustine's biased attitude had proved for free will. Evidently for the Jesuits this revival of interest in Augustine was a real thorn in the flesh! So they tried to show to whoever was prepared to listen to them that Jansen's book was, by any standards, a dangerously heretical work which fell, together with the works of Luther and Calvin, under the ban of the anathema, the curse pronounced by the Council of Trent.

By the same token naturally the whole circle of those connected with Port-Royal fell under the same condemnation. From then onwards, in France and elsewhere, Jansenism came to be regarded as an even more dangerous heresy than Lutheranism or Calvinism. They succeeded in persuading not only the King of France, Louis XIV, that this was the case, but also the pope and the Roman

Curia — with all the consequences that such a judgement
would bring in its train! The Augustinian revival, so full of
new life and promise, was mercilessly destroyed by sword
and by fire. All that remains of the Abbey of Port-Royal is
a ruin, which even today is still a place of pilgrimage for
French Catholics who join with Pascal in crying out in the
face of this horrible injustice, *'Ad tuum, Domine Jesu,
tribunal appello* — I appeal, Lord Jesus, to your judgement
seat!'⁸

So the *Augustinus* disappeared off the stage of church
history. On the final page of a little book on Port-Royal we
read, 'Port-Royal is no more. Where has anyone ever found
more sincere piety wedded to the most extensive knowledge,
or greater holiness of life associated with the greatest of
mental gifts and the most extraordinary qualities of
character? From the depths of the valley where the abbey
used to stand, a cry has gone up which will not be silenced,
similar to the call which Augustine in his day used as he
exhorted people to embrace the faith; the faith shared by so
many martyrs, the faith of people from every race and nation,
the faith of so many men, women, children and old people.
"How", this voice asked Augustine, "can you today fail to do
what they all did before you: give your heart to the one who
is your Lord, your Saviour, your Redeemer?" In its day,
Port-Royal proclaimed the same message. But Port-Royal is
no more. However, although Port-Royal has disappeared, its
memory is still very much alive. Every year large numbers
of people take an interest in it, come there on pilgrimage,
trample over the ruins, go all over this sacred site and still
discover among the ruins some sparks of the flame of faith
which once burnt there...'

The voice of Augustine, the preacher of grace, can no
longer be heard within the walls of the Roman church. After
all, if Rome were to endorse the message of Augustine, it
would also have to withdraw its condemnation of Luther and
Calvin! And that Rome could never do, because it would be
tantamount to admitting that the Council of Trent had made
a mistake!

Freedom in Jesus Christ

It is by grace alone that we are saved (Eph. 2:8-10). Calvin teaches: 'The beginning of goodness is from the second creation which is obtained in Christ. If any, even the minutest, ability were in ourselves, there would also be some merit.'[9]

In another place he says, 'In this way, then, man is said to have free will, not because he has a free choice of good and evil, but because he acts voluntarily, and not by compulsion. This is perfectly true.'[10]

The Bible says, 'You were slaves of sin' (Rom. 6:17). What grounds have we then for boasting of our free will? Similarly, the Bible teaches that we were 'dead in trespasses and sins', and that God made us alive 'because of his great love with which he loved us' (Eph. 2:1-10). 'Because of his great love', such is the teaching of the Word of God; it is not that he found anything in us which was receptive or favourably disposed towards his grace. For our old nature cannot be made better; it cannot be rehabilitated or 'patched up'.

In the epistle to the Romans Paul puts it like this: 'For to be carnally minded is death, but to be spiritually minded is life and peace. Because the carnal mind is enmity against God; for it is not subject to the law of God, nor indeed can be. So then, those who are in the flesh cannot please God' (Rom. 8:6-8). It is in Jesus Christ that we can enjoy the benefits of a new creation: 'If anyone is in Christ, he is a new creation; old things have passed away; behold, all things have become new' (2 Cor. 5:17). The Bible teaches us that the natural man does not have a free will, but a will which is in bondage, because he is subject to desires which dominate and enslave him.

Augustine asks, 'How can miserable human beings dare to claim that they have free will, before their will has even been set free, or how can they trust to their own strength, as if they were already free? They do not take into account that the very expression "free will" implies liberty. For where the Spirit of the Lord is, there is liberty.'

We may state clearly that human nature is totally blind towards God and that there is nothing in it which can bring it into a relationship with God. For man's whole will is totally opposed to God.

The *Canons of Dort* state this clearly as follows: 'But as man by the Fall did not cease to be a creature endowed with understanding and will, nor did sin which pervaded the whole race of mankind deprive him of the human nature, but brought upon him depravity and spiritual death; so also this grace of regeneration does not treat men as senseless stocks and blocks, nor take away their will and its properties, or do violence thereto; but it spiritually quickens, heals, corrects, and at the same time sweetly and powerfully bends it, that where carnal rebellion and resistance formerly prevailed, a ready and sincere spiritual obedience begins to reign; in which the true and spiritual restoration and freedom of our will consist. Wherefore, unless the admirable Author of every good work so deal with us, man can have no hope of being able to rise from his fall by his own free will, by which, in a state of innocence, he plunged himself into ruin.'[11]

Let me close this chapter with Article 14 of the *Belgic Confession of Faith*: 'We believe that God created man out of the dust of the earth, and made and formed him after his own image and likeness, good, righteous, and holy, capable in all things to will agreeably to the will of God. But "being in honour, he understood it not," neither knew his excellency, but wilfully subjected himself to sin and consequently to death and the curse, giving ear to the words of the devil. For the commandment of life, which he had received, he transgressed; and by sin separated himself from God, who was his true life; having corrupted his whole nature; whereby he made himself liable to corporal and spiritual death. And being thus become wicked, perverse, and corrupt in all his ways, he has lost all his excellent gifts which he had received from God, and retained only small remains thereof, which, however, are sufficient to leave man without excuse; for all the light which is in us is changed into darkness, as the Scriptures teach us, saying: "The light shineth in the darkness, and the darkness apprehended it not"; where John calls men darkness.

'Therefore we reject all that is taught repugnant to this concerning the free will of man, since man is but a slave to sin, and "can receive nothing, except it have been given him from heaven". For who may presume to boast that he of himself can do any good, since Christ says: "No man can come to me, except the Father that sent me draw him"? Who will glory in his own will, who understands that "The mind of the flesh is enmity against God"? Who can speak of his knowledge, since "The natural man receiveth not the things of the Spirit of God"? In short, who dare suggest any thought, since he knows that "We are not sufficient of ourselves to account anything as of ourselves, but that our sufficiency is of God"? And therefore what the apostle says ought justly to be held sure and firm, that "God worketh in us both to will and to work, for his good pleasure." For there is no understanding nor will conformable to the divine understanding and will but what Christ has wrought in man; which he teaches us, when he says: "Apart from me ye can do nothing."'

2.
The Roman Catholic view of grace

Rome has whittled away at all that God has revealed in his Word about grace until they are left with a whole series of subtle differences of meaning which can hardly be distinguished one from the other. Rome speaks of aiding, or actual, grace and sanctifying grace, of created and uncreated grace, of operating and co-operating grace, of prevenient grace and executing grace, of grace as a quality of being and as a quality of doing.

It is all rather like a skilfully woven piece of fabric which may be appreciated only by professional theologians. The sincere Catholic who takes his beliefs seriously feels confused, trapped in the web of all these arguments and, most serious of all, loses sight of the true way of salvation. Such subtleties of meaning are totally inadequate to convey to us anything of the infinite richness of the grace of God.

Sin

If we want to understand anything at all about grace, we must first have a correct view of sin. Anyone who is not convinced about sin can never taste the joy, nor experience the peace and confidence of a life transformed by grace.

Are we clear about what sin is in the sight of a holy God? I am firmly convinced that we shall never understand all the implications of the fact that God is 'of purer eyes than to behold evil'. I also believe that it will take us all our lives even to begin to appreciate the sinfulness of our own nature. The *Heidelberg Catechism* teaches that it is God's will 'that all our life long we may learn more and more to know our sinful nature, and so become the more earnest in seeking remission of sins and righteousness in Christ'.[1]

Sin is always the result of a positive choice on the part of man, a personal, conscious choice. This is why it is fundamentally a choice against God. God detests sin and sin is an insurmountable disaster for man. What ravages sin has caused in our relationship with God! We who, in ourselves, are nothing but pretentious human beings, have by our erring ways, denied, ridiculed and dishonoured the Most High, the holy God, Creator of heaven and earth.

How hard are our treacherous hearts, how full of evil tendencies and desires, and prone to every kind of wickedness! Read Genesis 3 at your leisure. Sin is not some kind of accident brought about inadvertently or by weakness, and which could consequently be put right by an appeal to the 'good' in us. No, sin consists of effectively turning away from God and the tendency to do so grows in us along with our own human nature. Our human race is by its very nature sinful, so that, of himself, man can only go on sinning more and more.

We believe that, through the disobedience of Adam, original sin has spread throughout the whole human race. It is a corruption of the whole nature and a hereditary evil, which taints even little children while still in their mothers' wombs and which, acting as a root, produces in man all kinds of sin. Consequently in God's sight it is so repulsive and outrageous that it is enough to condemn the human race, and it is not abolished or ever completely eradicated, not even, as Rome teaches, by baptism, since it is always breaking out again, like foul water bubbling up from a polluted spring.

The Bible teaches that man is spiritually dead because of sin. This fact too means that 'assisting' or 'co-operating' grace cannot possibly be sufficient (as Rome teaches). Only 'saving' grace leads to life.

'Be sure your sin will find you out,' says the Bible in Numbers 32. What a solemn warning this is! It is at the foot of the cross that we discover just how serious sin is. What anguish Jesus endured when he was abandoned by his God! How bitter was the cup that he drained: 'O my Father, if it is possible, let this cup pass from me'! With our distorted little understanding, we cannot possibly enter fully into all that Jesus experienced. How painful and oppressive his suffering must have been:

'He is despised and rejected by men,
A man of sorrows and acquainted with grief.
And we hid, as it were, our faces from him;
He was despised, and we did not esteem him'
(Isa. 53:3).

On the cross he cried out, 'My God, my God, why have you forsaken me?' Jesus, as a man, was rejected by God. He cried to God, but the Father did not listen to him! He was rejected by God and it was our fault! He was made sin for us (2 Cor. 5:21). He was willing to be stripped of all righteousness and honour! John 19:24, the passage where we read of the soldiers dividing up his clothes, speaks to us eloquently of how he laid everything aside on our behalf. Can you imagine Jesus, the Son of God, nailed naked on the cross of shame? How angry God must be against sin! Because of sin we have no rights at all. What an illustration of our misery! For our sakes, Christ had to lose everything, absolutely everything. And through his poverty, we became rich. Jesus, hanging naked on the cross, was cut off from the holiness of God. He hung there, in the presence of God, in all the nakedness of sin.

God is too holy to be able to look upon sin. So it is also God's holiness which causes him to say, 'Get out of my sight!' Here we see the horrible nature of sin and the inhumanity of our depraved condition. No man can stand upright in the presence of this all-revealing light. My heart breaks and, overcome with emotion, I weep at the foot of this cross. 'I am the one who sinned,' is all I can say at the sight of the holiness and righteousness of God. David used the same words, 'I have sinned,' when the prophet Nathan denounced his transgression of the law. Again and again the law points to us and says, 'You are the man!' The law shows us the ugliness of our sinful nature, our depraved state.

'Whence do you know your misery?' asks the Heidelberg Catechism, and gives the answer: 'Out of the law of God.'[2] And Paul tells us in Romans 3:20: 'By the law is the knowledge of sin.' The revealing light of the law makes us cry out:

> 'My sin is ever before me ...
> Behold, I was brought forth in iniquity,
> And in sin my mother conceived me'
>
> (Ps. 51:3-5).

It is therefore absolutely necessary not to lean on man for justification, but to turn away from looking at the sinful, guilty creatures that we are and to seize hold of the only justification which God accepts and which is revealed in the gospel of grace. 'How shall we escape if we neglect so great a salvation?' (Heb. 2:3). I ask you, how could we appear before God except through him? It is impossible!

We too must strip off our clothing, the garments woven by self-righteousness and sewn by pride, together with the deceit, the hardness of heart, the illusion of wisdom and the claims of self which we still try to put on in order to appear or to be something! The cross declares powerfully that no garment can hide our guilt. Neither the garment of penances, nor that of prayers, nor a robe of ritual, nor a cloak of tears, nor even conversion itself can cover us. Only the Christ who laid aside everything to hang on the cross can clothe us! Nothing that man can produce can appease the wrath of God. Only a perfect sacrifice could satisfy the righteousness of the almighty God.

In his confusion, the prophet Micah exclaimed:

> 'With what shall I come before the Lord,
> And bow myself before the High God?

Shall I come before him with burnt offerings,
With calves a year old?'

(Micah 6:6).

All that a man can do is not enough; it cannot satisfy God. Only the sacrifice of Jesus can perfectly satisfy God.

It was on the cross of shame that Jesus drank the cup of God's wrath to the last drop, so that we might drink the cup of salvation. It was because of his great love for the sinner that Jesus voluntarily trod this path, in submission to his Father's will, so that we should not be consumed by the fire of God's wrath, nor any longer have to pass through the floods of his judgement.

Sin is so hateful in God's sight that it can only lead to judgement and the eternal death of man. All calls to salvation are swallowed up by sin. Only grace can bring salvation. Anyone who still entertains doubts about this and who still thinks he is able to contribute anything at all offends the holy God and casts a shadow on the perfection of the work of salvation accomplished by Jesus Christ. Such a person has not yet reached the critical point in his life, where he recoils in horror from the sight of himself, as he appears in the light of the holiness of God.

Anyone who thinks that he can 'earn' or 'deserve' anything knows nothing of a deep sense of guilt. He does not know the 'godly sorrow' which Paul speaks of in 2 Corinthians 7:10. It is this godly sorrow alone that gives rise to joy in God. We can never know joy in God if we have not been touched by godly sorrow. 'For godly sorrow produces repentance [which leads] to salvation, not to be regretted; but the sorrow of the world produces death.' I believe that godly sorrow is real for anyone who claims to be a Christian. It is an actual sense of sadness, both on account of sin in our lives, but even more because of our fundamental need of the presence of God. This godly sorrow causes suffering in our hearts because of sin, because by it we have grieved the holy God.

The consciousness of sin leads us to the cross, which is a

painful testimony to the lack of God's presence. Calvin
writes, 'Hence, in respect, first, of our corrupt nature; and,
secondly, of the depraved conduct following upon it, we are
all offensive to God, guilty in his sight, and by nature the
children of hell.'[3]

'For, in order to remove our condemnation, it was not
sufficient to endure any kind of death. To satisfy [the
requirements of] our ransom, it was necessary to select a
mode of death in which he might deliver us, both by giving
himself up to condemnation, and undertaking our expiation.
Had he been cut off by assassins, or slain in a seditious
tumult, there could have been no kind of satisfaction in such
a death. But when he is placed as a criminal at the bar, where
witnesses are brought to give evidence against him, and the
mouth of the judge condemns him to die, we see him
sustaining the character of an offender and evildoer.'[4]

'The cross was cursed not only in the opinion of men, but
by the enactment of the divine law. Hence Christ, while
suspended on it, subjects himself to the curse. And thus it
behoved to be done, in order that the whole curse, which on
account of our iniquities awaited us, or rather lay upon us,
might be taken from us by being transferred to him.'[5]

The cross is also the most gracious testimony to divine
mercy. It proclaims God's sovereign grace: 'He
"condemned sin in the flesh" (Rom. 8:3), the Father having
destroyed the power of sin when it was transferred to the
flesh of Christ. This term, therefore, indicates that Christ, in
his death, was offered to the Father as a propitiatory victim;
that, expiation being made by his sacrifice, we might cease
to tremble at the divine wrath. It is now clear what the
prophet means when he says that "The Lord hath laid upon
him the iniquity of us all" (Isa. 53:6), namely, that as he was
to wash away the pollution of sins, they were transferred to
him by imputation. Of this the cross to which he was nailed
was a symbol, as the apostle declares, "Christ hath redeemed
us from the curse of the law, being made a curse for us: for
it is written, Cursed is every one that hangeth on a tree: that
the blessing of Abraham might come on the Gentiles through

Jesus Christ" (Gal. 3:13-14). In the same way Peter says, that he "bare our sins in his own body on the tree" (1 Peter 2:24), inasmuch as from the very symbol of the curse, we perceive more clearly that the burden with which we were oppressed was laid upon him. Nor are we to understand that by the curse which he endured he was himself overwhelmed, but rather that by enduring it he repressed, broke, annihilated all its force. Accordingly, faith apprehends acquittal in the condemnation of Christ, and blessing in his curse.'[6]

This cross has also become a reality in my own life. I can freely and in all humility testify to this since I experienced personally what it means to have died with Christ. His cross has assumed more and more significance in my life, until I can no longer escape this process of dying. The truth reveals my inflated ego for what it is, passes sentence on it and condemns it to death, so that grace can accomplish its work of renewal in my life. Jesus Christ has destroyed the power of this body of sin. I am no longer under law but under grace. This is our testimony as evangelicals. This is what we want to proclaim so that many may be 'cut to the heart' (Acts 2:37).

Rome's view of grace

In the following passage, I want to concentrate on two aspects of grace which Rome distinguishes very clearly one from the other. I want us to examine the concepts of 'sanctifying grace' and 'aiding' or 'actual grace'.

1. Aiding grace

According to the Malines Catechism, aiding grace is a temporary supernatural help, which enlightens our understanding and strengthens our will to do good and reject evil.[7]

This supernatural assistance is an immediate enlighten-
ment of the understanding and an immediate strengthening
of the will. The Roman teaching declares that, for every step
which brings us nearer to God and strengthens our bonds of
love with him (the way of sanctification), there must be a
direct action on the part of God. But does not the Bible teach
that a believer, through the new birth, partakes of the divine
nature? (2 Peter 1:4). We are a new creation (2 Cor. 5:17),
'the new man which was created according to God, in
righteousness and true holiness' (Eph. 4:24).

It is because of the blood of the Lamb that we can live in
communion with the Almighty. We have free access to the
sanctuary (Heb. 10:19). Because of the covenant of God's
grace, we live in a situation in which communion with God
is always possible, the relationship is always open. God does
not need to come back each time. He did it once for all in the
sacrifice of Jesus Christ. 'For by one offering he has
perfected for ever those who are being sanctified' (Heb.
10:14). On the basis of his perfect sacrifice and his
intercession as the great High Priest, we are kept unto
salvation by the power of God! 'Now may the God of peace
himself sanctify you completely; and may your whole spirit,
soul, and body be preserved blameless at the coming of our
Lord Jesus Christ. He who calls you is faithful, who also will
do it' (1 Thess. 5:23-24). His is abundant grace! (Rom. 5:20-
21).

This aiding grace is also subdivided into 'operating
grace', 'co-operating grace' and 'superior grace'.

Operating grace

Rome teaches that 'There is a supernatural action of God on
man's psychology which precedes all decisions of free will.'
Thus Rome teaches that the origin of sanctification is in God;
the source of the first steps leading us towards God lies in the
power of God. After that the will, which has been
strengthened, must continue by itself to go forward on the

way of sanctification. This is where Catholicism finds itself in an impasse: everyone receives enough strength to sweep his own doorstep and clear the pavement outside his house. But the Bible never mentions an operating grace which helps us to make progress in even the smallest degree. On the contrary, the Bible speaks of a grace which saves. According to Rome, sanctification is a human activity, maintained with God's help. This teaching is not biblical. I shall have more to say about this point later.

Co-operating grace

God and man work together. The work of sanctification which takes place is the fruit of co-operation between the grace of God and the human will. Grace sustains and leads the actions of human free will. Rome teaches (at the Council of Trent, for example) that the sinner prepares his conversion *'gratiæ libere assentiendo et cooperando'*, which means that he freely approves and freely co-operates with grace.

On this subject they quote 1 Corinthians 15:10: 'By the grace of God I am what I am, and his grace toward me was not in vain; but I laboured more abundantly than they all, yet not I, but the grace of God which was with me.' Rome sees a certain synergism in this text: grace works with Paul and Paul works with grace, and so we can see the spectacular results of his work. This explanation contradicts what Paul was trying to say. He wanted to show precisely that it is purely grace, and grace alone, which allows him to bear fruit.

We can see from other passages that this was what Paul meant. In 2 Corinthians 3:5 it is spelt out clearly: 'Not that we are sufficient of ourselves to think of anything as being from ourselves, but our sufficiency is from God.'

All Rome's pronouncements on the subject of grace are infected with the idea of the 'ability to act by the power of grace'. On this topic, we shall quote once more from the Council of Trent: 'To all believing sinners, God gives enough grace *(gratia saltem remote sufficiens)* to enable them to be converted.'

'With God's help, a sinner can and should prepare to be in Christ.' Is not this preparation too the work of God? It is the Holy Spirit who convicts of sin, righteousness and judgement (John 16:8).

An article in the Roman Catholic magazine *Waarheid en leven* (July-August 1987) shows us that Rome has not changed in its teaching about grace: 'When a man co-operates with this grace, he concentrates all his energy on living and working for God. In doing so he will call down upon himself even greater grace, for God never lets himself be outdone by noble feelings. In this way the Christian will become more and more like God.

'When a man reaches such a state of dependence on God, in his heart and soul, that in all conscience he recognizes that it is by love for God that he works and lives for the salvation of his neighbour, then sanctifying grace is abundant and the man approaches perfection and holiness.

'The more like God man is and the more he strengthens the bonds of friendship and love between himself and God, the more God will love him. For the person who possesses a high degree of sanctifying grace is by virtue of that very fact that much more closely united with God. He therefore deserves the love of God and of men more intensely than does the person who after his baptism just takes life as it comes. The freedom of the will to co-operate is always present; it can be accepted or rejected. Man is not able to approach God without the aid of assisting grace. He will never attain to likeness to God and achieve perfection without divine help. Indeed, this is all a very difficult process, even with God's help. So we can say with St Paul, "It is no longer I who live, but Christ who lives in me."'

Surely this makes man in some sense a partner with God in the work of salvation? If only man could see that if God's salvation had to rely, even fractionally, on our co-operation with grace, no salvation would be possible. God saves on the basis of grace and not on the basis of some good will on our part!

Sanctifying grace

Question 148 of the *Malines Catechism* teaches: 'Sanctifying grace is a supernatural and permanent quality given to our souls which makes us partakers of the divine life. It sanctifies us and makes us children of God and heirs of heaven.' This statement gets to the very heart of the teaching of the Roman Catholic Church about sanctification.

In the *Catholic Catechism for Adults*, Rome acts as if there were practically no difference between Catholic and Protestant views of justification: 'The ecumenical dialogue of the last decade has made a lot of progress in teaching about justification. Many Catholic and Protestant theologians agree now that this teaching should not be a cause of division between the two churches, and that it is possible to give an answer to this question which will satisfy both sides. The Catholic teaching and Protestant teaching about the relationship between grace and works are not contradictory or mutually exclusive; it is true that they are not altogether the same, but they do have something in common, they can remain open to each other.'[8]

It seems that when it comes to the content of the teaching there is not all that much difference, and the variations are only superficial! Nothing could be further from the truth! It is a fundamental difference. In fact it is a question of either 'sovereign grace' or 'merits by the power of grace'. It is a question of either living by God or by the flesh. It finally comes down to either believing or working. The former leads to eternal glory, the latter to eternal destruction.

The desire to minimize in this way the unique and perfect character of the sacrifice of Jesus on the cross can only be the work of an 'evil spirit of ecumenism'. I want first of all to state very plainly that the gospel categorically denies the existence of any merit which could have connection with our justification before God.

The pronouncements of the Council of Trent on the subject of justification describe it as 'a translation from that state in which man is born as a child of the first Adam, into the state of grace, and of the adoption of the sons of God'.[9] At the basis of this statement is the idea of grace which calls those who through sins are turned away from God, without the existence of any merits on their part, and disposes them to turn themselves unto their own justification by a voluntary co-operation and free assent to this grace.[10]

They do not speak so much of faith as of 'trust'. Faith is described as an act of the understanding which approves what God has revealed: 'The faith which is at the origin of human salvation is a supernatural virtue by which we believe that what God has revealed is true.' That is how it was defined by the First Vatican Council.

Grace is therefore considered as the 'beginning' of the way of salvation. That implies that, according to Rome, faith is not a decisive or dominating factor (otherwise faith is no longer faith), but rather a certain stage in the way of salvation. It is found at the very beginning of the path which leads man to salvation. For Rome, faith is the initial impetus which makes communion with God possible. Faith is not therefore saving unless it becomes a faith which has taken shape, that is, which has been formed by love.

Thus faith becomes a question of human performance, a participation by man, which becomes a decisive factor in justification. Yes, and behind all that, we see constantly lurking the shadow of human merit.

'So we arrive at an astounding declaration: if faith is "something", it has a certain degree of merit. If faith is "everything", then it has no merit at all. If faith is "something", then we are co-workers with the power of grace. If faith is "everything", we can only be recipients of the word of grace, which offers us and gives us everything that we need to appear before God, in his presence, and to live by him.'[11]

Infused righteousness

The Council of Trent declared that 'If anyone shall say, that by faith alone the impious is justified; so as to mean that nothing else is required to co-operate in order unto the obtaining the grace of justification, and that it is not in any respect necessary that he be prepared and disposed by the movement of his own will; let him be anathema!'[12]

The Bible teaches that we are saved *freely*, by *grace*, by *faith*. However, Rome pronounces a curse on those who teach that justifying grace is purely and simply a gift of God. Rome denounces as accursed all those who teach that justifying faith is none other than trust in the mercy of God, who is willing to pardon sins because of Christ! So it is that Rome distances itself from the biblical truth of salvation by grace alone and faith alone *(sola gratia, sola fide)*. In doing so Rome distances itself from the only basis of salvation! To speak of a justification which is infused into grace is to cast a slur on the character of grace.

We need to grasp the significance of this. This grace which is 'infused' is an 'indispensable justification'; the nature of God and his virtues are infused into man by means of the sacrament of baptism. Rome does not speak of a justification by imputation, but of an actual transformation: we become righteous. The *Catholic Catechism for Adults* tells us, 'So the justification of God transforms man in a real and true way. Justification is not simply a declaration of his righteousness, but it accomplishes justification in the man. It changes and renews him. This leads to two consequences: the pardon of sins and the "sanctification and renewal of the inner man" (DS 1528) This justification is therefore also a sanctification by which we have, in the Holy Spirit, communion with God through Jesus Christ.'[13]

The Council of Trent is also very clear on this point: 'Justification ... is not merely the remission of sins, but also the sanctification and renewal of the inward man, through the voluntary reception of the grace and gifts, whereby man from unjust becomes just, and from an enemy a friend...'[14]

'The sole formal cause [of justification] is the justice of God; not that by which he himself is just, but that by which he maketh us just, that, to wit, with which we, being endowed by him, are renewed in the spirit of our mind, and we are not only reputed, but are truly called, and are, just, receiving justice within us...'[15]

Calvin is correct when he says, 'I place it [justification] outside of ourselves, for in Christ we are all justified.' The Bible does not speak of justification in terms of a transformation, but of a justification which has been imputed and given (Rom. 4). That means a person is considered as righteous, declared righteous before God. It is not a question of infusing a righteousness which makes man righteous in himself, but of declaring someone to be righteous through faith (Rom. 4:4-8).

Calvin teaches on this subject: 'In the same manner, a man will be said to be *justified by works*, if in his life there can be found a purity and holiness which merits an attestation of righteousness at the throne of God, or if by the perfection of his works he can answer and satisfy the divine justice. On the contrary, a man will be *justified by faith* when, excluded from the righteousness of works, he by faith lays hold of the righteousness of Christ, and clothed in it appears in the sight of God not as a sinner, but as righteous. Thus we simply interpret justification, as the acceptance with which God receives us into his favour as if we were righteous; and we say that this justification consists in the forgiveness of sins and the imputation of the righteousness of Christ.'[16]

He goes on to say, 'To *justify,* therefore, is nothing else than to acquit from the charge of guilt, as if innocence were proved. Hence, when God justifies us through the intercession of Christ, he does not acquit us on a proof of our own innocence, but by an imputation of righteousness, so that though not righteous in ourselves, we are deemed righteous in Christ. Thus it is said in Paul's discourse, in the Acts, "Through this man is preached unto you the forgiveness of sins; and by him all that believe are justified from all things from which ye could not be justified by the law of Moses" (Acts 13:38-39). You see that after remission of sins justification is set down by way of explanation; you see plainly that it is used for acquittal; you see how it cannot be obtained by the works of the law; you see that it is entirely through the interposition of Christ; you see that it is obtained by faith; you see, in fine, that satisfaction intervenes, since it is said that we are justified from our sins by Christ.'[17]

Rome declares that sanctifying grace has made me so perfect and good that on that basis I am capable of building a life which is pleasing to God. I am henceforth capable of doing so. On the basis of grace, I have been given the capacity to acquire merit before God. So I can assert my rights before him. Man is so deeply and really transformed by this infused grace that he now has the power of pleasing God. Man is therefore no longer acceptable to God on the grounds that God sees him in Christ and grants him the righteousness of Christ, but apart from the work of Christ, man becomes good. Grace is no longer considered as a gift of God outside of man himself, but as a supernatural force which elevates our human nature to a higher level, to a divine level, so that the new man is able to build up a store of merit before God.

Existential elevation

Rome speaks of an existential elevation which makes man capable of earning heaven. What is this existential elevation? I will try to explain this point by the use of an illustration. Suppose that you have a pet dog. Like all dogs, he has a nature which is subject to the limitations of an animal and his experience of happiness is also limited to certain spheres of existence. Happiness for your dog means basking in the sun or chewing a bone. It has never occurred to a dog that happiness could mean anything else. Yet there are other sources of happiness. For example, you, as his owner, have other ideas of what it means to be happy. Human beings, unlike dogs, may find pleasure in reading a good book, or in the nature which God has created, or in listening to music, in friendship or being in love. But imagine that you were in a concert hall, listening to a Beethoven symphony and that you were suddenly to say, 'I wish my dog could be here to be able to enjoy the concert.'

The next time, you take him along with you, and when the orchestra plays, your dog starts howling. How could it be otherwise? For your dog to be able to appreciate music as you do, it is not enough just to take him to the place where you appreciate it. You would have to impart human qualities to your dog; he would have to some degree to share in human nature. You would have to give him a new life which could transport him onto a higher plane, you would have to be able to raise him to a higher level of existence.

This is the reasoning adopted by Rome when it comes to the relationship between man and God. God's happiness is on a totally different plane from what we humans could imagine. God wants us to be able to enjoy it with him. But for that to be possible, it is not enough just to move us to heaven, as it were. Our nature being what it is, we should be at least as bored in heaven as a dog would be in a concert hall. Why? Because by nature we could not know the happiness that God knows. God's happiness is far above our capacity for happiness. God would have to plant divine qualities in us, make us partake of his divine nature, raise our whole existence onto a higher plane.

According to Rome, that is exactly what God does through the sacrament of baptism. This confers sanctifying grace, that is, the life of the new birth. That is the teaching of Rome about justification. That is what I was taught as a student, chiefly through reading a book which was recommended to us at the time, *Christen Nu,* by Dankelman. This teaching is still regarded as authoritative today.

Rome does not teach a justification by faith in the redeeming work of Christ, but speaks of an actual righteousness in man which becomes a separate element in his make-up. If we take this line of thought to its logical conclusion, the man who is justified in this way can claim the actual 'justification of his being' as something which he possesses personally.[18]

This is where the fundamental difference lies between Rome and the Reformation. It is not just some minor detail; it concerns the very heart of the gospel — the sovereign character of the grace of God which is denied by the teaching of an 'infused righteousness'.

Rome teaches that by infused righteousness (baptism as practised by the Roman Catholic Church) man is renewed and becomes righteous. The basis on which God is satisfied is no longer to be found in Christ, but in the transformed man himself. The transformation of a sinner into a righteous man is the work of Christ, by his sufferings and death. But when the sinner who has been justified once and for all on the basis of the work and merits of Jesus Christ has become a righteous man, then, according to Rome's teaching, God is satisfied not because of a righteousness which is external to the man and imputed to him, but because he takes pleasure in the man himself. This is one of the terrible consequences of this teaching of 'infused righteousness'. Oh that eyes may be opened, and that people might see what the Bible teaches on this subject! The Bible shows up the teaching of the Council of Trent as a deliberate distortion of the gospel.

The Bible teaches that man is and remains a sinner and that he will never find in himself anything at all that can be pleasing to God! If God looks on us outside of Christ, he can only judge and condemn us. The only basis for acceptance with God is Jesus Christ, the 'Beloved Son', with whom he was well-pleased. It is at this point that we can speak of predestination — a predestination that originates in God alone and can never depend on anything at all in man.

'The good pleasure of God is the sole cause of this gracious election; which does not consist herein that out of all possible qualities and actions of men God has chosen some as a condition of salvation, but that he was pleased out of the common mass of sinners to adopt some certain persons as a peculiar people to himself, as it is written: "For the children being not yet born, neither having done anything good or bad, ... it was said unto her" (namely, to Rebekah), "The elder shall serve the younger. Even as it is written, Jacob I loved, but Esau I hated" (Rom. 9:11,12,13), "And as many as were ordained to eternal life believed" (Acts 13:48).'[19]

Rome claims that the cause lies partly in ourselves, by the righteousness which was conferred on us, and by which we are inwardly transformed (born again), and thus become acceptable to God.

The Bible teaches us that the basis of our justification is outside ourselves, that its origin is the will of God, and that it is based on the grace revealed in Jesus Christ.

A work of refined sanctification

Calvin expresses himself forcefully on this subject: 'But as Osiander has introduced a kind of monstrosity termed *essential righteousness*, by which, although he designed not to abolish free righteousness, he involves it in darkness, and by that darkness deprives pious minds of a serious sense of divine grace; before I pass to other matters, it may be proper to refute this delirious dream ... he had formed some idea akin to that of the Manichees, desiring to transfuse the divine essence into men.'[20]

What is the crux of the problem here? It is a very serious matter to oppose in this way all that the Bible tells us, as Rome does, and to cling to one's own teaching, that of infused grace. I say it again, according to Rome, justification is not on the basis of the reconciliatory work of Jesus Christ, even though the Council of Trent declares that Jesus was 'set forth' by God 'as a propitiator', and that 'through faith in his blood'.[21] This teaching about infused righteousness fails to recognize Jesus as the only mediator. This teaching is ungodly. I find this deeply distressing. Can they not see that this teaching denies that Christ is our righteousness?

Calvin continues: 'And [Osiander] vehemently asserts ... that Christ is himself our righteousness, not in so far as he, by expiating sins, appeased the Father, but because he is the eternal God and life.'[22]

Calvin understood better than any this subtle and yet very important distinction between Roman Catholic teaching and biblical truth on the subject of justification. I will leave the final word on this particular point to him: 'But although he pretends that, by the term essential righteousness, he merely means to oppose the sentiment that we are reputed righteous on account of Christ, he however clearly shows, that not contented with that righteousness, which was procured for us by the obedience and sacrificial death of Christ, he maintains that we are substantially righteous in God by an infused essence as well as quality. For this is the reason why he so vehemently contends, that not only Christ but the Father and the Spirit dwell in us. The fact I admit to be true, but still I maintain it is wrested by him. He ought to have attended to the mode of dwelling — viz. that the Father and the Spirit are in Christ; and as in him the fulness of the Godhead dwells, so in him we possess God entire. Hence, whatever he says separately concerning the Father and the Spirit, has no other tendency than to lead away the simple from Christ. Then he introduces a substantial mixture, by which God, transfusing himself into us, makes us as it were a part of himself. Our being made one with Christ by the agency of the Spirit, he being the head and we the members, he regards as almost nothing unless his essence is mingled with us. But, as I have said, in the case of the Father and the Spirit he more clearly betrays his views — namely, that we are not justified by the mere grace of the Mediator, and that righteousness is not simply or entirely offered to us in his person, but that we are made partakers of divine righteousness when God is essentially united to us.'[23]

Why am I giving so much attention to this subject? First of all, because Jesus Christ's perfect work of reconciliation is arrogantly cast aside and replaced by so-called human merits. In the last analysis this would mean that man could be saved without the intervention of Jesus Christ! How could a man, who in his heart is capable of the worse atrocities, ever satisfy a holy God? Did Christ go to the cross in vain? 'I do not set aside the grace of God; for if righteousness comes through the law, then Christ died in vain' (Gal. 2:21). These words show the utter futility of any human effort to please God.

This is why it seems to me to be profitable to deal with the subject at length, not only because to allow any credence to this aspect of Roman Catholic teaching obscures the character of God's grace, but because it lies at the root of a superficiality in our consecration to the Lord in all its simplicity. Only faith in the sovereign grace of God keeps us persevering in the way of faith. Read Hebrews 11 if you have any doubts about this.

It is sometimes said that Rome's teaching is not all that far removed from that of the Bible. Rome acknowledges Jesus as the Son of God and as Saviour. But we need to realize that the Roman Catholic teaching is based on a presupposition which is opposed to that of the Bible, that of merits on the basis of a kind of grace. Have we fully appreciated the consequences of such a teaching? Anyone who follows this way will inevitably come to have a sense of the value of his own efforts and his own accomplishments and pride will then creep in under cover of this. There is an element of pride in all that is taught about human merits. It is true that this teaching starts with an undeserved grace, but as it goes on, it builds up a structure based on merits.

However, the truth of God calls us to turn away from all reliance on our own abilities. The gospel takes no account of anything that man does of himself. Rome talks in terms of grace (sanctifying grace and infused righteousness), but at the same time its work of refined sanctification strikes a mortal blow at the teaching of the grace of God.

Sanctification is the work of God

Rome says that justification is the work of God, but that sanctification is principally a human work. Once justified, man must continue by himself on the way of sanctification, with the assistance, of course, of efficacious grace. Bavinck rightly teaches: 'There are many who acknowledge that they are justified by the justification obtained by Christ, but who imagine, or at least live in practice as if their sanctification depended on their own efforts.'[24] So man is pointed back to the law again! Such are the inevitable consequences of the Catholic teaching about justification.

However, the Bible teaches very clearly that Christ became for us, because of God, wisdom, righteousness, sanctification and redemption (1 Cor. 1:30). This text shows clearly that sanctification too is given freely to us. Sanctification is not, as some say, a virtue which we can appropriate to ourselves with the help of Christ; no, sanctification is a gift made to us by Christ. He himself is our sanctification. It is impossible for us to accomplish it by ourselves.

The Bible specifically tells us that man is sanctified by God: 'Now may the God of peace himself sanctify you completely ...' (1 Thess. 5:23).

The Bible speaks equally plainly of man's involvement in the process of sanctification. Our life as believers, like that of the people of Israel (Lev. 19), is rooted in the fact that we belong to God. On the basis of this truth and of the fact that we serve a holy God, we are called to live in holiness.

Indeed, this is the clear message of the New Testament. Paul challenges us: 'How shall we who died to sin live any longer in it?' (Rom. 6:2). He asks the believers at Corinth, 'Do you not know that your bodies are members of Christ?' (1 Cor. 6:15), or again, 'Do you not know that your body is the temple of the Holy Spirit who is in you ... and you are not your own? For you were bought at a price; therefore glorify God in your body and in your spirit, which are God's' (1 Cor. 6:19-20).

We should not take this to mean that we must henceforth make a special effort to improve our way of life so as to attain to a higher moral plane. No, if that were so, we should still be doing our best, we should be engaged in a kind of spiritual 'do-it-yourself'. But Paul tells us in Romans 6:22, 'But now having been set free from sin, and having become slaves of God, you have your fruit to holiness, and the end, everlasting life.' Sanctification is called a fruit. It is a fruit which is bound up with the service of God; just as the bondage to sin bore fruit in death, so sanctification is inseparably linked to the service of God. There is a close link between the two, which resembles the intimate connection between the seed and the fruit. Anyone who tries to speak of his own accomplishments and merits on the way of salvation finds his claims totally refuted by Paul in this passage. It concerns a growth which did not originate in us and the development of which we are unable to control. This process, which affects us, calls for a response on our part and we have a share of responsibility for it, but we are not the ones who cause the fruit to ripen; it is God who gives the increase (1 Cor. 3:6).

Our sanctification is based on the holiness of God. It is on the basis of divine mercy that we are called to live as those who are holy. The believer's sanctification can therefore never be grounded in any human activity, independent of the work of God in us.

Calvin had understood what Paul meant when he wrote, 'We are not our own; therefore, let us not make it our end to seek what may be agreeable to our carnal nature. We are not our own; therefore, as far as possible, let us forget ourselves and the things that are ours. On the other hand, we are God's; let us, therefore, live and die to him (Rom. 14:8). We are God's; therefore, let his wisdom and will preside over all our actions. We are God's; to him, then, as the only legitimate end, let every part of our life be directed. Oh how great the proficiency of him who, taught that he is not his own, has withdrawn the dominion and government of himself from his own reason that he may give them to God!'[25]

My dear reader, do you now understand a little better the deep need of the Catholic? While giving lip-service to the grace of God, he is still under the yoke of the curse of the law. This thought cuts me to the heart. It is a satanic lie in the Roman Catholic system which prevents men from obtaining eternal salvation. I would like to be able to cry out, 'No! Tell me it's not true! It can't be!' Yet in the light of the Word of God I cannot see how it can be otherwise. O church of Rome, church of Rome, turn to the God of free grace, enter into the rest of true gospel freedom!

3.
The value of good works

I want to start this chapter with a few quotations from Calvin. We shall see that he had to fight hard to be totally free from the system of works, which is the foundation stone of the whole structure of Roman Catholicism.

As I read these profoundly moving lines from Calvin's writings, I often see myself in them: 'Whenever I came to a deeper understanding of myself, or when I lifted my thoughts towards you, I was terrified. The more clearly I came to know myself, the more my conscience was wounded and torn apart. The only solution left to me was to ignore the situation and deceive myself. I couldn't see any alternative. This was my state of mind as I carried on with the route I had mapped out for myself.

'In the meantime, a very different teaching had come to light. Far from leading us astray from the Christian faith, it brought us back to its source and delivered it from all impurity, restoring it to its original purity. But the novelty of this teaching proved a stumbling-block to me and I found it hard to listen.

'At first, I admit, I was violently opposed to this teaching. The main reason was the tenacity, or rather the stubbornness, with which men are prone to cling to what they have once learned. On the other hand, I was loth to admit that up until that time I had been living my whole life in ignorance and error. There was one thing which especially made me hold back, and that was respect for the church. But once I was able to pay attention and receive the teaching, I understood that this fear of casting aspersions on the church's honour was groundless, for I realized the great difference between the person who deliberately distances himself from the church and the one who tries to repair the breaches in its walls or to purify it from its stains.'

So we see that fear of impugning the honour of the church can prevent a man from coming to the truth. It was this same respect for the Roman Catholic Church which for many years prevented me from seeking the salvation which is found in the truth of God's Word. The truth of Scripture has convinced me, too, of the vanity of the Catholic teaching about the 'meritorious nature of good works'.

On the one hand, Rome teaches the absolute impossibility of any human being saving himself and the absolute need of salvation through Jesus Christ. The Council of Trent underlines this point: 'If anyone shall say, that man may be justified before God by his own works, whether done through the strength of human nature, or through the teaching of the law, without the divine grace through Jesus Christ; let him be anathema.'[1]

On the other hand, Rome teaches that works accomplished in a state of grace have a 'meritorious' and 'redeeming' power. The Roman Catholic catechism says that 'We are obliged to accomplish good works to earn heaven.' The Council of Trent also supports this statement: 'If anyone shall say, that a man who is justified and how perfect soever, is not bound to the observance of the commandments of God and of the church, but only to believe; as if, forsooth, the gospel were a bare and absolute promise of eternal life, without the condition of observation of the commandments; let him be anathema.'[2]

'If anyone shall say, ... that the [man that is] justified, by the good works which are performed by him through the grace of God and the merit of Jesus Christ, whose living member he is, does not truly merit increase of grace, eternal life, and the attainment of that eternal life...; let him be anathema!'[3]

But such teaching is not scriptural! The Scripture teaches: 'For by grace you have been saved through faith, and that not of yourselves; it is the gift of God, not of works, lest anyone should boast. For we are his workmanship, created in Christ Jesus for good works, which God prepared beforehand that we should walk in them' (Eph. 2:8-10). In this passage Paul wants to make it clear that it is completely impossible to imagine that we can deserve anything from God because of our good works. Good works are not accomplishments which we can put forward in our favour, but they are the work of God in us!

Rome is fond of quoting Matthew 19:17, where Jesus tells the rich young man, 'If you want to enter into life, keep the commandments.' At first sight, this statement by the Lord Jesus does seem to confirm the teaching of merits. But what did the Lord Jesus mean by this statement? He wanted to teach the rich young man, and if we look at the context, we can see how, and with what knowledge of the human heart, he knows how to speak to men. They met on the basis of the law and it is on the basis of the law that Jesus answers his questions. So, meeting him on his own ground, Jesus wants to make him understand and feel his need, for what did this young man need? He needed first of all to realize his state of being a lost sinner, in grave danger. Only the law could show him his true situation. Jesus helps him to realize that it is impossible to enter the kingdom of God by one's own efforts. Salvation comes from God; it is a grace in Jesus Christ (Matt. 19:20-26).

Rome also declares that 'Good works have in them a power which enables us to gain heaven. Salvation is not therefore solely and uniquely the work of God's grace; it is not only the product of grace, but it is also a product of merits.'[4]

The Council of Trent teaches: 'Unto them who work well unto the end, and hoping in God, life eternal is to be proposed, both as a grace mercifully promised to the sons of God through Jesus Christ, and as a recompense which is to be faithfully rendered to their good works and merits according to the promise of God himself.'[5]

This statement is a reaction to Question 63 of the *Heidelberg Catechism*, which teaches: 'This reward is not of merit but of grace.' In an attempt to support its statement, Rome quotes Matthew 25:21: 'His lord said to him, "Well done, good and faithful servant; you were faithful over a few things, I will make you ruler over many things. Enter into the joy of your lord."' Rome sees here a relationship of cause and effect between good works and salvation. Augustine, on the other hand, teaches: 'When man discovers that all the good that he possesses does not come from himself, but from God, he will discover that everything in him which is praiseworthy has its origin not in his merits, but in the grace, the mercy of God.'

The idea of reward

The idea of reward is clearly a biblical concept: 'Whatever you do, do it heartily, as to the Lord and not to men, knowing that from the Lord you will receive the reward of the inheritance; for you serve the Lord Christ' (Col. 3:23-24). 'For God is not unjust to forget your work and labour of love which you have shown toward his name, in that you have ministered to the saints, and do minister' (Heb. 6:10). '... esteeming the reproach of Christ greater riches than the treasures in Egypt; for he looked to the reward' (Heb. 11:26; see also Rev. 20:12; 11:17-18; 1 Cor. 3:8).

In the Bible there is no idea of merit in this concept of a reward. In the Bible the reward cannot be compared to a relationship such as exists in the field of economics: it is not a contractual response to some accomplishment on the part of the believer. The Reformers were right to draw attention to Luke 17:10 whenever this subject was raised: 'So likewise you, when you have done all those things which you are commanded, say, "We are unprofitable servants. We have done what was our duty to do."' Jesus takes away any idea of personal merit!

Professor Greijdanus writes in his commentary on this verse, 'We belong wholly and utterly to God, and believers are wholly owned by the Lord Jesus because of his redemptive work. It is to him that they owe all that they are, all that they have in abilities, gifts, possessions, time and circumstances — they receive it all from God by his creation and providence. They therefore owe everything to God and are incapable of doing anything which they are not already required to do. Thus it is not possible for them to accomplish anything more than what they owe to God, which could bring him any profit, or any additional accomplishment for which God could thank them. That is totally impossible. The Lord is teaching here that all that we accomplish has absolutely no meritorious value, even if we were to accomplish everything that he has commanded. God has a right to everything. It is absolutely impossible to accomplish more good works than God asks of us; consequently it is impossible for us to rely on them to receive any thanks or any reward.'

Article 24 of the *Belgic Confession of Faith* is also very clear on this: 'Nevertheless, [good works] are of no account towards our justification, for it is by faith in Christ that we are justified, even before we do good works; otherwise they could not be good works, any more than the fruit of a tree can be good before the tree itself is good.

'Therefore we do good works, but not to merit by them (for what can we merit?); nay, we are indebted to God for the good works we do, and not he to us, since it is he who "worketh in us both to will and to work, for his good pleasure". Let us therefore attend to what is written: "When ye shall have done all the things that are commanded you, say, We are unprofitable servants; we have done that which it was our duty to do." In the meantime we do not deny that God rewards good works, but it is through his grace that he crowns his gifts.

'Moreover, though we do good works, we do not found our salvation upon them; for we can do no work but what is polluted by our flesh, and also punishable; and although we could perform such works, still the remembrance of one sin is sufficient to make God reject them. Thus, then, we would always be in doubt, tossed to and fro without any certainty, and our poor consciences would be continually vexed if they relied not on the merits of the suffering and death of our Saviour.'

The Council of Trent also says of works that they are accomplished by the grace of God. However, the teaching on grace in the church of Rome is a synthesis of grace and liberty, and the idea of reward will always suggest an element of human worth and therefore be threatening for the teaching of justification by grace alone. Besides Rome attaches great importance to the uniqueness of the man who receives as of right the fruit of his labour, the reward. The fact that man has received everything from God, just as a child receives everything from its father, makes man incapable of giving to God anything which belongs to him personally. God has given to man the ability to perform good works, and God will also give him the fruit of his works, a sort of reward, or wages. Why does Rome reckon it to be so? Because in God's way of acting in relation to our acts there must be a certain characteristic: that of responding to a certain 'personalization' of our own actions.

When a mathematician attempts to solve a problem, or a farmer cultivates the ground, or when a mother gives birth to a child, we can only speak of the 'fruit' of their labours in terms of what they have invested in it. We can only say their efforts are rewarded to the extent of this investment on their part. However we try to explain it, I cannot get away from the idea that according to Rome, there is a certain aspect of God 'owing' something to man.

Reward on the grounds of promise

It was Calvin who made the famous statement that 'The kingdom of heaven is not the hire of servants, but the inheritance of sons.'

Calvin also refers to the promise to Abraham that his descendants would be as numerous as the sand on the seashore: 'Many years after he prepares, in obedience to a divine message, to sacrifice his son. Having done this act of obedience, he receives the promise, "By myself have I sworn, saith the Lord, for because thou hast done this thing, and hast not withheld thy son, thine only son; that in blessing I will bless thee, and in multiplying I will multiply thy seed as the stars of the heaven, and as the sand which is upon the seashore, and thy seed shall possess the gate of his enemies; and in thy seed shall all the nations of the earth be blessed, because thou hast obeyed my voice" (Gen. 22:16-18). What is it we hear? Did Abraham by his obedience merit the blessing which had been promised him before the precept was given? Here assuredly we see without ambiguity that God rewards the works of believers with blessings which he had given them before the works were thought of, there still being no cause for the blessings which he bestows but his own mercy.'[6]

It seems to me that this point is very important if we are to understand the correct meaning of the word 'reward'. The reward can never be separated from the free grace and mercy of God. But divine mercy includes God's grace. The one who believes in Jesus Christ will never be able to earn anything, for the reward is based on the promises and when we receive something solely because someone else promised it, we can never speak of having earned it. We can speak in terms of perseverance in waiting for the accomplishment of the promise, without there being any merit involved; that is what receives the reward.

Calvin goes on: 'And yet the Lord does not act in vain, or delude us when he says, that he renders to works what he had freely given previous to works. As he would have us to be exercised in good works, while aspiring to the manifestation, or, if I may so speak, the fruition of the things which he has promised, and by means of them to hasten on to the blessed hope set before us in heaven, the fruit of the promises is justly ascribed to those things by which it is brought to maturity. Both things were elegantly expressed by the apostle, when he told the Colossians to study the offices of charity, "for the hope which is laid up for you in heaven, whereof ye heard before in the word of the truth of the gospel" (Col. 1:5). For when he says that the gospel informed them of the hope which was treasured up for them in heaven he declares that it depends on Christ alone, and not at all upon works.'[7]

We can think of the reward as the revelation of God's mercy: 'Let us always remember that this promise [Heb. 6:10], like all other promises, will be of no avail unless it is preceded by the free covenant of mercy, on which the whole certainty of our salvation depends.'[8]

If there was any way in which we could earn our salvation, then it would not have been necessary for Jesus to come into this world and Golgotha would have been a disastrous mistake! Anyone who claims that he can earn salvation because of the 'power of grace' in him treats the work of Christ with contempt and sets out on a path utterly rejected by the gospel.

In the *Augsburg Confession*, we read that works have no power to reconcile us to God or to acquire a special grace. This can only be obtained by faith, if we believe that our sins are forgiven because of Christ, the only mediator between the Father and us (1 Tim. 2:5). Anyone who claims that he can receive these gifts by means of good works, and so can deserve grace, only pours contempt on the work of Christ and seeks to reach God in his own way. This is contrary to the teaching of the gospel.

For grace to remain grace, we must not try to turn it into anything else. All our human merits only cast a shadow on the glory of the merciful grace of God. Paul says, 'If by grace, then it is no longer of works; otherwise grace is no longer grace' (Rom. 11:6). It is nothing more nor less than grace! Our works, even the best of them, are too imperfect to be able to claim anything at all. Even our prayers are marred by pride.

Luther used to say about good works and their meritorious value, 'It is the devil himself who talks of the merits of good works, but it is not a frightening devil, dressed all in black, or in lurid colours, but a devil clad all in white who, under cover of a pious disguise, claims to offer you eternal life as he invites you to drink poison and death.' Further on he says, '"The just shall live by faith" (Rom. 1:17) does not mean that the just man does not do any works, but they are not works which are capable of justifying him; rather it is his justification which produces the works.'

Good works as the fruit of faith

Rome often refers to James 2:14-26 and says, 'You see, good works are important, for it is written in black and white that Abraham was justified by his works. So it is obvious that man is justified by works and not by faith alone.'

At first sight, this passage from the epistle of James appears to contradict Paul's statement in Romans 4:3 that 'Abraham believed God, and it was accounted to him for righteousness.' James, for his part, refers to Genesis 22, where Abraham offered up his son Isaac: 'Was not Abraham our father justified by works when he offered Isaac his son on the altar?' (James 2:21).

James says of this action, 'And the Scripture was fulfilled which says, "Abraham believed God, and it was accounted to him for righteousness." And he was called the friend of God' (James 2:23). This verse shows clearly that this act on the part of Abraham was a work of faith, the fruit of his faith. James sees in this incident the fulfilment of the words quoted in Genesis 15:6. Faith is made perfect by action. We may draw the inference that James sees a very close link between faith and works. He sees the life of Abraham as a whole. He does not think of it only from the time when Abraham believed in Genesis 15:6, but he sees that Abraham's whole life was comprised of works which were the fruit of his faith. The one who believes also performs works. However, these works do not justify him; rather, they are the expression of his faith. So James sees here the fulfilment of the word quoted in Genesis 15:6; this word is as it were brought out into the open, made perfect, completely fulfilled and given concrete form by Abraham's obedience in Genesis 22.

He says it equally clearly in verse 22: Abraham's faith was 'made perfect' by his works. That does not mean that Abraham's faith was at first imperfect and lacking in some way, but that the quality of Abraham's faith was revealed by his sacrifice.

James also tells us that Abraham's faith was 'working together with his works'. In other words, Abraham's faith and his works were inseparably linked. When one was in action, the other was equally active.

How then can anyone take this to mean that James sets works alongside faith as an additional element in justification? Anyone who says this shows that he has not understood what James is saying here in chapter 2. I would like to refer to Professor Berkouwer's book, *Faith and Justification,* on this point.

There is no doubt that the Bible teaches that good works are pleasing to God, but they do not in themselves possess any power to purify us. It is 'by faith' that we are justified before we have ever performed any good works. Calvin writes on this subject, 'As justification, if dependent upon works, cannot possibly stand in the sight of God, it must depend solely on the mercy of God and communion with Christ, and therefore on faith alone... It is certain that, being a high-sounding term, [merit] can only obscure the grace of God, and inspire men with pernicious pride... Such, however, is our malignity, that, not contented with this liberality on the part of God, which bestows rewards on works that do not at all deserve them, we with profane ambition maintain that that which is entirely due to the divine munificence is paid to the merit of works.'[9]

What, then, is the basis of our justification? When, in the light of the holiness of God, we discover our own worthlessness and lukewarmness, we are distressed by the feeble quality of our life, by the self-centredness which persists in raising its ugly head and boasting of its fleshly achievements. We can only remain silent when we realize that all our good works can never be a solid foundation on which to base our justification, for even the very best of our actions is still reprehensible in the sight of the holy God.

Let us take heed of the witness of the Holy Spirit in Romans 8, who tells us that all our actions are polluted, being in bondage to corruption. And that is true even of our very best actions. All we can do is blush with shame and despair and cry out with Isaiah,

> 'Woe is me, for I am undone!
> Because I am a man of unclean lips...
> For my eyes have seen the King'
>
> (Isa. 6:5).

But, 'Oh, the depth of the riches both of the wisdom and knowledge of God! How unsearchable are his judgements and his ways past finding out!' How vast the richness of God's grace! We are in the presence of the Holy One and we cannot utter a single word, such is our amazement and wonder. Our hands are empty. That is how we stand before the holy God. On what foundation dare we appear before him? On what basis can we come into the Holy of Holies?

Will we come on the basis of our piety? Will we trust the fact that we read the Bible, or that we are faithful in our personal devotions? If we were to do so, that would be worth nothing in God's sight. Paul goes so far as to describe these things as rubbish. Only the blood of the Lamb is a solid foundation. On the basis of the blood of the Lamb, we may stand before God. He is the Lamb who was sacrificed on our behalf.

> 'Worthy is the Lamb who was slain
> To receive power and riches and wisdom,
> And strength and honour and glory and blessing!'
>
> (Rev. 5:12).

Jesus Christ is the only true foundation: 'For no other foundation can anyone lay than that which is laid, which is Jesus Christ' (1 Cor. 3:11). It is his perfection which is given to us by faith: 'For by one offering he has perfected for ever those who are being sanctified' (Heb. 10:14).

What grounds does anyone have, then, for boasting? 'But of him you are in Christ Jesus, who became for us wisdom from God — and righteousness and sanctification and redemption — that, as it is written, "He who glories, let him glory in the Lord"' (1 Cor. 1:30-31).

Once again, let me quote Calvin: 'What then is our foundation in Christ? Is it that he only opened up the way, and left us to follow it in our own strength? By no means, but as Paul had a little before declared, it is to acknowledge that he has been given us for righteousness. No man, therefore, is well founded in Christ who has not entire righteousness in him, since the apostle says not that he was sent to assist us in procuring, but was himself to be our righteousness. Thus it is said that God "hath chosen us in him before the foundation of the world" not according to our merit, but "according to the good pleasure of his will"; that in him "we have redemption through his blood, even the forgiveness of sins"; that peace has been made "through the blood of his cross"; that we are reconciled by his blood; that, placed under his protection, we are delivered from the danger of finally perishing; that thus engrafted into him we are made partakers of eternal life, and hope for admission into the kingdom of God. Nor is this all. Being admitted to participation in him, though we are still foolish, he is our wisdom; though we are still sinners, he is our righteousness; though we are unclean, he is our purity; though we are weak, unarmed, and exposed to Satan, yet ours is the power which has been given him in heaven and in earth, to bruise Satan under our feet, and burst the gates of hell (Matt. 28:18); though we still bear about with us a body of death, he is our life; in short, all things of his are ours, we have all things in him, he nothing in us. On this foundation, I say, we must be built, if we would grow up into a holy temple in the Lord.'[10]

In my opinion, Rome has never really understood the teaching of the Reformation about justification by faith alone. According to Rome it is a transaction which does not have any actual results, or effect any change in the man. In fact the contrary is true: faith is the very soil in which love and good works can blossom and that is possible because, by the grace of God, this faith touches our lives and gives them worth. So only the person who is justified by faith is in a position to perform good works. Why? Because works cannot be pleasing to God unless they are performed on the basis of his grace.

'Where is boasting then? It is excluded. By what law? Of works? No, but by the law of faith. Therefore we conclude that a man is justified by faith apart from the deeds of the law' (Rom. 3:27-28).

'Who can deny that men are labouring under a kind of delirium, when they suppose that they procure eternal life by the merit of their works?' wrote Calvin to the Emperor Charles V and those assembled with him at the Diet of Spires. 'I admit that they conjoin the grace of God with their works, but in as much as their confidence of obtaining acceptance is made to depend on their own worthiness, it is clear that the ground of their confidence and boasting lies in their works. The trite and favourite doctrine of the schools, the opinion deeply seated in almost all minds, is — that every individual is loved by God in exact proportion to his deserts. Entertaining this view, are not souls, by means of a confidence which the devil inspires, raised to a height, from which, as from a loftier precipice, they are afterwards plunged into the gulf of despair? Again, when they pretend to merit the favour of God, it is not merely by true obedience, but by frivolous observances, of no value. The meritorious works to which the first place is assigned are these — to mumble over a multitude of little prayers, to erect altars, and place statues or pictures thereon — to frequent churches, and run up and down from one church to another — to hear many masses, and to buy some — to wear out their bodies, by I know not what abstinences — abstinences having nothing in common with Christian fasting; and, in particular, to be most careful in observing the traditions of men. In the matter of satisfactions, is it not even a greater infatuation which makes them, after the manner of the heathen, set out in quest of expiations, by which they may reconcile themselves to God?

'After all these attempts, after great and long fatigue, what did they gain? Doing every thing with a dubious and trembling conscience, they were always exposed to that fearful anxiety, or rather that dire torment, of which I have already spoken, because they were enjoined to doubt whether their persons and their works were not hateful to God. Confidence being in this way overthrown, the necessary consequence was, as Paul declares, that the promise of the eternal inheritance was made void. In such circumstances, what became of the salvation of men?

'Where there was such necessity for speaking, had we kept silence, we should have been not only ungrateful and treacherous towards God, but also cruel towards men, over whom we saw eternal destruction impending, unless they were brought back into the proper path.'[11]

4.
Indulgences

I still remember very clearly how, as a little boy, I used to go to church every year with my father, on a particular day, for something called the 'portiuncula'.

This involved some very odd goings-on. People were coming in and going out of the church all the time, and what I really found puzzling was that it was the same people who kept on coming in and going out. My father told me that people could earn a plenary indulgence by doing this. First of all you had to confess your sins to the priest in the confessional, then after having received absolution for your sins and having prayed five Paternosters, five Ave Marias and five Glorias, you went out of the church and came back in again; and so you earned an indulgence. This ceremony was repeated over and over again. The more times you did it, the more indulgences you could gain. This indulgence was called 'the Indulgence of the Portiuncula'.

What was the origin of this indulgence? The Portiuncula was a place in Italy, where there was a small chapel in the woods commemorating the place where St Francis of Assissi had settled with his companions. They built little huts of wood and dried earth, because Francis didn't on any account want to give it the character of a permanent home. He wanted the brothers to be ready to move on at any time wherever God might call them.

One night in the summer of 1216, St Francis got up in the night to go and pray in the chapel of Portiuncula. While he was praying, he saw a vision of Jesus Christ, who is supposed to have told him to go to the pope and ask that all those who went to the chapel of Portiuncula after having been to confession should receive a plenary indulgence, that is, the pardon of all temporal penalties for their sins.

St Francis went to the pope, who at the time was Honorius III, and asked him, 'If it please your holiness, I should like all who go to this church after they have made confession, repented and been absolved by the priest, to receive pardon for all their sins, in heaven as well as on earth, from the day of their baptism up to the day when they cross the threshold of this church.' The pope gave his consent and from that day on, this plenary indulgence was handed out at the Portiuncula.

It is helpful if we understand how a tradition such as this came to be built up around the life of St Francis of Assisi. St Francis was a man who had on his heart the salvation of sinners. When, at the Fourth Lateran Council of 1215, he heard the terrible threats pronounced by Innocent III against the Waldensians and Albigensians and other sects, he was filled with great compassion for the world and so he appealed to the pope to recognize the indulgence of the Portiuncula. The pope applied the words of Ezekiel 9 to himself and used this passage to organize a crusade against Jerusalem and also to make certain reforms in the church, regarding himself as being the man 'clothed with linen', with 'a writer's inkhorn at his side' (Ezek. 9:2-3).

He explained the passage in this way and declared that God had told him, 'Go through the midst of the city, through the midst of Jerusalem, and put a mark on the foreheads of the men who sigh and cry over all the abominations that are done within it' (v.4). His audience were described as the 'six men' who 'came from the direction of the upper gate, which faces north...' and they received from their leader the command: 'Go after him through the city and kill; do not let your eye spare, nor have any pity. Utterly slay old and young men, maidens and little children and women; but do not come near anyone on whom is the mark' (the letter T in the shape of a cross).

They were to fight with all their strength, they were empowered to declare people outlaws, to suspend, excommunicate them or divest them of their office, until the city was purified. St Francis was horrified by the pope's interdict and sought a means of 'bringing God's forgiveness more quickly to repentant souls'. This 'means' was to be the indulgence of the Portiuncula.

The history of indulgences

The teaching and practice of indulgences did not exist in the early days of Christianity; it developed little by little. The Council of Trent promulgated a dogma which is still regarded as authoritative in the Catholic Church, to the effect that the church had the power to grant indulgences.

In the first centuries of the history of the Christian church, canonical penalties consisted of excluding people from religious practices and from the fellowship of the church. In certain special cases, bishops had authority to shorten the length of time for which a penalty was applied. This shortening of a sentence was in a fact a remission of the penalty. This was one aspect of what later developed into the indulgence.

Early church discipline punished severely those who denied their faith as a result of persecution and those who were guilty of serious misdemeanours. The person who had publicly denied God was to be punished by standing at the church door for seven consecutive Sundays, with a cord round his neck, and the last Sunday he had to go barefoot as well. He also had to fast on bread and water for seven consecutive Fridays. A son who cursed his parents had, as a punishment, to fast for forty days on bread and water. Premeditated murder was punished by excommunication and the guilty person could not receive the holy sacrament from the altar except on the day of his death. The punishment for adultery lasted from seven to ten years. There was also a whole scale of penalties for less important sins.

If someone was carrying on a conversation during the mass, he would only be sentenced to ten days' fasting on bread and water. After that he was considered to have put things right with the church and he could take part in the eucharist. From the earliest days, we find cases where the guilty person was pardoned before the whole of the penalty had been carried out. Indeed people who distinguished themselves by their zeal in carrying out their penance could be pardoned after a certain period of time had elapsed. These rules were defined by the Councils of Ancyra (314) and Nicæa (325). Offenders could also be reconciled with the church at the request of martyrs, whose suffering and death were considered to possess an expiatory value sufficient to make payment in the place of the guilty person.

In the seventh and eighth centuries, it was comparatively rare to punish someone by way of example to others. There were what were called 'redemptions' or 'ransoms'. These appeared first in Ireland and England at the end of the seventh century. From there they spread over more or less the whole of Europe.

Instead of severe penalties, redemption could be obtained by means of prayers, pilgrimages or almsgiving. So it was decided, for example, that one day of strict fasting was valued at one 'denarius'. One prayer uttered on one's knees was worth the same as fifty psalms. One prayer uttered while standing upright was worth seventy psalms, or feeding three poor people, or receiving a beating of fifty strokes. There were many abuses to the system and all too often someone else was punished in place of the offender.

We can see in all this the same spirit as that which inspired indulgences. All these meritorious actions were mitigations of the punishment and thus a partial remission of guilt in God's sight.

At about the same time, the idea developed of redemption by payment of money. A person could make expiation by investing a certain sum of money in some good work or other. Little by little, the element of redemption became less important and the role of the church in granting the pardon became more and more crucial.

By the time we reach the eleventh century, it seems that

this type of redemption had disappeared and, by that very fact, the indulgence seems to have taken on its definitive shape. As far as we know, the earliest indulgence dates from 1063. It was issued by Pope Alexander II for the benefit of the Spaniards who were fighting against the Moors. In 1095, Pope Urban II gave a full indulgence to those who took part in the crusades. He declared, in a letter addressed to the clergy at Bologna, that all those who took part in the crusades where absolved from all sins that were confessed in due form.

In addition to this pardon, there was also a change in the way punishment was carried out. This is confirmed by the pronouncements of the Council of Clermont (1095), which said that, by their crusades, the crusaders deserved a full and total remission of punishment. Similar statements can be found in the last papal bulls on the subject of the crusades.

In was in the year 1300 that the Jubilee Indulgence was issued by Pope Boniface VIII. At first it was confined to Rome and could be renewed every hundred years. Later it underwent various changes as to time and place.

The indulgence for the dead dates from the fifteenth century and was issued by Popes Callistus III and Sixtus IV.

There were terrible abuses. 'Quæstors' (from the Latin *quærere*, to ask for alms) were appointed to bring in the money demanded by the popes and bishops in order to qualify for their indulgences. These men sold indulgences, extolling them highly and declaring them to be absolutely necessary for salvation. Pope Paul III tried in 1546 to put a stop to these illegal practices.

Money was not required for a partial indulgence, but for plenary indulgences a fixed price had to be paid. I quote from Cardinal de Jong's *Manual of Church History*: 'How much did believers have to pay? For partial indulgences, money was not normally required; for plenary indulgences, money was usually required. For the Jubilee Indulgences, at the time of Nicholas IV, the sum required was the equivalent of half or a quarter of the price of a journey to Rome. The poor had to pay their financial debts by prayers. In the second half of the eleventh century, the standard used in the church was the sum needed to live for a week. According to the *Instructions of Mainz*, in 1517, kings, queens, archbishops, bishops and other high-ranking nobles were to pay, for the Indulgence of St Peter, twenty-five golden florins of the Rhineland Palatinate. Abbots and other dignitaries, counts, barons and other noblemen, were to pay ten florins. Less exalted prelates, the rest of the nobility and all those who had an annual income of 200 florins, were to pay six florins. The middle classes, the merchants and other craftsmen, were to pay one florin or half a florin.

'The preachers of indulgences could not leave the poor out of this trade, "seeing that the salvation of believers is no less important than the building of St Peter's Church. Those who have no money are to build up for themselves a treasure of prayers and fasting; seeing that the kingdom of heaven is open equally to rich and poor alike."

'So it was a question of trying to obtain money from pious men, and when that was not possible, it had to be replaced by prayer and fasting. The instructions were as follows: "Those are to be classed as poor who either have to beg for a living or who can only earn enough by their work to meet their daily needs, and who cannot therefore save anything." If someone brought a gift it was to be in a closed box.'[1]

In 1506 Pope Julius II (1503-1513) wrote an indulgence in connection with the building of the Basilica of St Peter. At the time, Roman architecture was flourishing and it was the same in the fields of painting and literature. He himself laid the foundation stone of St Peter's, which had been designed by Bramante, who was also the architect of the Vatican Palace. Michelangelo was given the responsibility of the frescoes for the Sistine Chapel and for the statue of Moses. Raphael was made responsible for the well-known fresco in the Stanza of the Vatican. All this cost vast sums of money.

His successor, Leo X, wanted to make an even bigger name for himself as a patron of the arts. He had a court of 638 persons of various rank; ranging from archbishops with responsibility to care for the poor, to elephant trainers, court musicians and even a court jester. He was also very fond of hunting and often went off on hunting trips for several weeks at a time, when he would be accompanied by 200 horsemen, including cardinals, musicians and actors. It was often the need for more money which prompted the popes to promote the trade in indulgences.

With the project for the construction of St Peter's, Julius II had set on foot a tremendous undertaking for which he needed vast sums of money. In 1510 he published a bull promising an indulgence *'in forma jubilæi'* to all those who could support his project financially. Four types of indulgences were sold. The most common were the following:

1. A plenary indulgence for all sins committed. This included the sufferings of purgatory. To obtain this, after having made confession, you had to testify to the sincerity of your repentance in at least seven churches bearing the papal insignia, and in each of these churches you had to say five Paternosters and five Ave Marias. In addition, you had to pay a sum of money which could be anything from one to twenty-five golden florins.

2. The total remission of all sins for souls already suffering in purgatory. You could buy this pardon with a sum of money calculated according to the financial status of the heir who wanted to free his ancestor's soul from purgatory. The cardinals and bishops agreed to take on the responsibility of raising this money for the pope, on condition that they would be assured of retaining their sees, with the possibility of an extension of their territory. This was how the trade in indulgences continued to grow. The bishops put pressure on the priests to invite preachers of indulgences, even at the expense of their own income.

The mirror of the popes

To give an idea of the different kinds of abuse which existed in the church, I quote from the book *The Mirror of the Popes* by Corvin Wierbitsky (published 1848). This book was banned by the Catholic church.

'In Germany there were more than 200 images of Mary. Pilgrims flocked to visit these "miracle-working statuettes". In Europe they numbered about 1200 (this was another way of obtaining indulgences).

'Pilgrimages were also made to the places where certain holy relics where kept and put on display. This brings us to the subject of relics. They were used as a way of persuading gullible people to part with their money.

'The most precious treasures were kept at Aix-la-Chapelle. Beside the most amazing spiritual riches there were also a whole range of diverse objects, such as for example, a huge robe said to belong to Mary, the swaddling clothes worn by the infant Jesus, coloured with a yellow pen to show where the baby had soiled them, and the cloth on which the head of John the Baptist had been placed. Attractions of this type brought as many as 142,000 pilgrims to Aix-la-Chapelle in 1496. In 1818 there were only 40,000, but in 1845 once again a million pilgrims went to Trêves to kiss an old smock, because it was obviously Christ's tunic, the one that the soldiers drew lots for at the foot of the cross. This tunic caused caused great excitement, generating a lot of heat as well as causing great delight. Several very learned men used all their expertise to try to prove that the Holy Tunic of Trêves was in no way superior to the twenty other such robes which already existed.

'Another important source of revenue was the handing out of "pallia". Pallium was the name given by the Romans to the robe worn by the Greeks. The emperors used to give this garment to the patriarchs or bishops to signify their approval and as a sign of friendship. Pope Gregory I had the idea of sending a pallium to all the bishops in return for a payment of 30,000 florins. Later the bishops had to go personally to get their pallium. John VIII declared that any archbishop who did not come to Rome for his pallium within a period of three months would immediately be dismissed. 30,000 florins for a cloak! Yet still all this income was not enough for the pope. The pallium shrank rapidly and took the form of straps. These garments were made by nuns from wool which had been blessed.

'Each archbishop had to buy a new pallium. Seeing that they were usually old men, who had frequently to be replaced, this became a very important source of revenue. A bishop who was transferred to another diocese also had to pay. Archbishop Markulf of Mainz had to sell the left leg of a statue of Christ in gold to pay for his pallium.

'The pope was holding a knife at the throat of the bishops and they in their turn held a knife at the throat of the faithful. They were sheep who were to be shorn as soon as a little wool could be seen.

'Meals held by Pope Sixtus IV (1471-1484) often cost 20,000 florins a time. But that did not matter because he fed only on the sins of Christians. He was very skilled in the art of finding money. He gave permission to the cardinals to commit the most flagrant carnal excesses during the months of July and August in exchange for the payment of significant sums of money. So Rome became filled with brothels. These brought in to the church 40,000 ducats a year. This income was recorded under the title of "tax on milk".

'Pope Boniface VIII had a "golden idea". A pilgrimage to Rome would be worth a plenary indulgence for all the sins committed in the whole of one's life, even including killing one's father or incest with one's own mother. In the year 1300, 200,000 foreigners went to Rome.

'Pope Clement decided that a century lasts too long and declared a jubilee year every fifty years. Pope Urban VI shortened this by seventeen years and made a jubilee every thirty-three years, in memory of the age of Jesus Christ. Sixtus IV shortened this period to twenty-five years because of the brevity of human life. Anyone who died on the journey to Rome went straight to paradise, declared Clement VI in 1350, and his soul would not make a stop in purgatory. Two priests took it in turns to man St Paul's altar in Rome by day and night. They were equipped with a whole set of croupier's instruments to collect the money which poured in. But still it was not enough. As the saying goes, "Priests, monks and hens are never satisfied."

'Boniface IX decided that many believers were not going to Rome because they could not afford the journey, so he found a solution. He sent out monks who gave plenary indulgences to those who paid one third of the cost of the journey.

'The trade in indulgences grew at an unprecedented rate under Leo X. New sources of revenue were created. One was the annates, by which the bishops' revenue for their first year in office went to the pope. The charges for a dispensation owed by priests who were too young were also to be paid by those who did not want to fast or by members of the same family who wanted to marry. The definition of the family was for this reason extended by the pope to include the tenth degree. So a person could have as many as 16,000 family members.

'By paying enough for a dispensation, it was possible to get out of going to the crusades. John XXII drew up a very precise list, setting out the various possibilities of dispensation and absolution.

'As we have seen, before the time of Leo X, the income was still insufficient. His children, mistresses, relations, jesters, actors and his love of the arts swallowed up huge sums of money, and the Holy Father was in debt. So a tax was introduced for the war against the Turks. This was a favourite pastime of the popes and a system of begging which had been well organized to finance the building of St Peter's. Anyone who paid the tax was given an indulgence.

'The Christian world was divided into different sectors. The centre for commerce sent out officials who were authorized to sell indulgences. I think that at this point I should quote the actual wording of these indulgences: "In the name of our Holy Father, the representative of Jesus Christ, I declare you absolved from all ecclesiastical punishment which you may have incurred, as well as any crime or offence which you may have committed up until now, however important it may be, as well as every sin which the pope alone has power to forgive, inasmuch as he possesses the keys of Holy Mother Church.

"'I free you wholly from all these punishments which would normally consign you to purgatory. I restore you to the communion of the church and of believers and I put you once again in the same position of purity and innocence as you were after baptism, so that at your death, the gates of hell, through which people pass to be punished, may be closed to you and that you may go straight to paradise. If your death does not take place immediately, this grace remains your inalienable possession."

'The price of such an indulgence varied. It depended on how serious the sin was. There was an official document which listed every conceivable kind of sin and the corresponding sum of money. The murder of a father or brother, incest, infanticide, divorce or adultery, unnatural relations, perjury, etc. — there was a well-defined tariff for everything. In exchange for a payment of ten ducats the clergy could get away with committing adultery, divorce, incest or with having relations with animals. But worst of all was what was written at the bottom of the list of prices: "Such graces cannot be given to the poor, for they have no money. They cannot therefore share in this comfort." And the money continued to pour into Rome.

'Leo X decided it would be a good idea to farm out some districts for a certain sum of money. Large landowners were made responsible for this and so the contents of everyone's purse, whether full or half empty, were emptied into the papal coffers. These farmers were not the most honest of men. For example, Count Albrecht of Brandenburg, a man who was by nature inclined to dishonesty, showed little confidence in his farmers and made them swear not to cheat their landlord. One of the farmers was the Dominican monk Johannes Tetzel, a Doctor of Theology. He was a jolly character who went from one market to another like a clever tradesman vaunting his wares. He had among his luggage a casket decorated with the papal insignia and he used to sing enthusiastically,

"As soon as the coin in the coffer rings,
The soul from purgatory springs."

'To attract people, he would talk a lot of nonsense, which
was not always very reverent. He could not only forgive sins
which had actually been committed, but also the sins which
people intended to commit. His impudence knew no bounds.
In Switzerland he gave absolution to a rich farmer who had
committed murder. The farmer told him that he had another
enemy whom he wanted to kill. He received permission to do
so in exchange for the payment of a modest sum.

'There were still other indulgences (which had to be paid
for, of course) so as to be entitled to kiss sacred relics.
Albrecht of Brandenburg had a valuable collection of relics.
He had some of them brought from Halle to Mainz. Amongst
these were some very unusual objects: hairs (eight in all)
belonging to the Virgin Mary, some of her milk, the gown in
which she gave birth to Jesus, and half of one of St Paul's
jaws, with four teeth.

'Indulgences have survived right down the years. They
still exist in the Roman church, although they are applied
today in a less crude and less public way than of old. The
Vatican now has other more numerous and more refined
sources of income. It used to be measured in billions; today
it still amounts to billions. What was this money used for? It
was used at the pleasure of a single man in Rome, who has
as much to do with us as the Mikado of Japan and who has
as much right to call himself the vicar of Christ as you and
I have — the tremendously wealthy deputy of a man who
himself had nowhere to lay his head! All of this gives rise to
feelings of disgust and shame.'

Luther

The trade in indulgences gradually developed into an
enormous ecclesiastical and economic swindle, to the
detriment of the proclamation of the gospel of grace. The

spiritual leaders shamelessly took advantage of man's innate need of certainty with regard to his position before God and the future eternal destiny of his soul. Indeed, I believe the problem of assurance in the matter of the soul played a crucial role in all this. According to Rome, it is possible for someone to commit a mortal sin and to live in a state of mortal sin. The burning question was, and still is, 'Can a man who is in that state still hope in the grace of God? Is there a way back?'

This is where people were cruelly misled. Luther himself fought to the very last ditch against doubt when this question came home to him personally. Luther came to recognize this horrible fraud for what it was and in the Word of God he found the certainty that all human merit is totally inadequate. It was on the basis of that Word that he fought with all his might against the trade in indulgences. The whole country was being exploited by preachers of indulgences like Johannes Tetzel, and the princes were responsible for ensuring that the money was indeed forwarded to Rome!

In 1530 Luther addressed an *Exhortation* to the clergy assembled at the Diet of Augsburg, in which he reminded them: 'Have you ... forgotten how my teaching was at first so precious to almost all of you? Then all the bishops were very glad to see the tyranny of the pope restrained a little, since he handled the endowed foundations too severely. Then they could watch me politely, listen, sit quietly, and be on the lookout how they might regain once more their entire episcopal authority. Then Luther was an excellent teacher who attacked indulgences so honestly... Luther was the "dear boy". He swept the chapters and parishes clean of such huckstering, held the stirrups for the bishops to enable them to remount, and threw a stumbling-block into the road for the pope.'[2] Luther warned people against the lies told by Tetzel.

He warned against the lie perpetrated by indulgences in his Ninety-five Theses, which he nailed to the door of the chapel of Wittenberg on 31 October 1517. I shall return in more detail to the subject of these theses in the following chapter, but I would first of all like to make the following remark: Luther could perhaps be accused of not distancing himself far enough from the pope and of attaching too great importance to man's repentance at the expense of the merits of Christ. That may be true, but we need to realize the tremendous explosion which followed in favour of the gospel of grace. Luther did not count the cost; he was ready for anything in order to save the treasure of the church, to defend the gospel of the grace and glory of God. Luther also went through difficult times in this process of liberation from the Catholic system of personal justification.[3]

Professor W. van't Spijker is right when he says in his book *Luther, promise and experience*, 'But the ecclesiastical battle over indulgences was necessary for the powerful, as it were explosive, revelation of his convictions: we are justified freely, by grace alone.'

The teaching of the Roman Catholic Church on indulgences

Question 135 of the catechism used in the Belgian dioceses asks the question, 'What is an indulgence?' and gives the answer: 'An indulgence is the pardon given by Holy Church of the temporal penalties which are our lot here below or in purgatory, after we have received the pardon of our sins.'

Question 136 asks, 'How can we earn indulgences?' and answers, 'To earn an indulgence, a person must be in a state of grace and fulfil the conditions taught by Holy Church.'

The word 'indulgence' comes from the Latin word *indulgencia* and means the pardon or the mitigation of a certain penalty. It is sin which is at the root of guilt and of punishment. The punishment incurred by sin can have two consequences: eternal and temporal.

The *New Catholic Catechism for Adults* teaches on this subject: 'For a better understanding of the teaching on indulgences which lies behind the practice of selling indulgences we need to realize first the two consequences of sin: on the one hand, sin forms a barrier to our relationship with God and leads to the loss of eternal life (eternal punishment); on the other hand, sin mars communion between man and God, it mars the man's personal life and relationships with his fellow men (temporal punishment). God does not impose these two penalties on us arbitrarily; they are inherent in sin itself. The forgiveness of sin and the restoration of communion with God are linked to the pardon of eternal punishment. The temporal penalties still remain. The Christian must therefore do his best to bear patiently suffering, hardship and troubles and to face death with patience, to perform works of mercy and love, to pray, and in various ways express his repentance, so as to put off the "old man" and put on the "new man".'[4]

So Rome teaches that this act of putting off the 'old man' and putting on the 'new man' is something that man does himself. That is not what the Bible teaches. Paul teaches in the epistles to the Colossians and the Ephesians that he considers the putting off of the old man and putting on of the new man to be a *fait accompli* (Col. 3:9-10). This putting off and putting on in fact took place at the new birth.

Professor S. Greijdanus writes the following in his commentary on the epistle to the Ephesians: 'So we must understand the apostle's words as a statement of fact; they have stripped off their old clothes, they have been renewed and reclothed. That is why in their daily life they must no longer behave like pagans, but they must let it be seen clearly that they are men who have been renewed.' And the fact that this is seen in our lives should not be attributed to man; that too is the work of God. It is the Holy Spirit who accomplishes this in us.

Rome also teaches that by means of the confessional and a perfect repentance, forgiveness is offered with regard to eternal punishment in hell and the guilt of sin, but that does not affect the temporal punishment which can still remain in force even after the sins have been forgiven. The Council of Trent teaches that 'It is absolutely false, and alien from the Word of God, that the guilt is never remitted by the Lord, without the whole punishment also being pardoned.'[5] As for the remission of remaining temporal punishment, the Catholic believer has two means at his disposal: the practice of good works and the merit of indulgences.

So the indulgence is 'a remission before God of the temporal punishment due to sins whose guilt has already been forgiven'.[6] It amounts therefore to a pardon offered by the church alongside the sacrament which is given by applying merits contained in the 'treasure of the church'. Rome teaches that this 'treasure of the church' is the sum of the merits acquired by Christ and the saints, especially Mary. The distribution and application of this stock of spiritual merits is the prerogative of the church. It is she who dispenses them, by means of the sacraments, but also in other ways, the most important of which is by means of indulgences.

In his *Apostolic Constitution Promulgating the Revision of Sacred Indulgences* (1967), Pope Paul VI made a statement about this 'treasure of the church'. He said, 'We certainly should not think of it as being the sum total of the material goods which have accumulated during the course of the centuries. On the contrary the "treasury of the Church" is the infinite value, which can never be exhausted, which Christ's merits have before God... In Christ, the Redeemer himself, the satisfactions and merits of his Redemption exist and find their efficacy. This treasury includes as well the prayers and good works of the Blessed Virgin Mary. They are truly immense, unfathomable and ever pristine in their value before God. In the treasury, too, are the prayers and good works of all the saints, all those who have followed in the footsteps of Christ the Lord and by his grace have made their lives holy and carried out the mission the Father entrusted to them. In this way they attained their own salvation and at the same time co-operated in saving their brothers in the unity of the Mystical Body.'[7]

For a 'plenary indulgence', which, according to the latest ruling on indulgences, can only be earned once on any given day, the following conditions apply: the required work must be performed (e.g., going to church, reciting the Lord's

Prayer or the confession of faith); going to confession; receiving communion; prayer for the pope's intentions (these conditions may be fulfilled before or after the work is performed, but it is recommended that they be on the same day); being free from all attachment to any sin at all, even venial sin.

Even today the practice of qualifying for indulgences is still something which is very much alive. On the occasion of All Saints' Day, the priest of the village where I was born appealed to the villagers to obtain a plenary indulgence. He had an article published in the local paper which he gave out with the parish magazine: 'Today, a visit to the church or the public chapel can enable you to obtain a plenary indulgence for the dead, by reciting the Lord's Prayer or the Confession of Faith.' Anyone who supposes that the practice of indulgences is a thing of the past is seriously mistaken.

There are two types of indulgence given by the Roman Catholic Church: the 'plenary' indulgence, by which all of the temporal punishment due to sin is removed; and the 'partial' indulgence, by which only a part of the temporal punishment is removed.

Up until 1967 partial indulgences used to be measured in days or years. What was an indulgence of 100 or 500 days? It did not mean — as is sometimes thought — that the time spent in purgatory was reduced by 100 or 500 days, but rather that by such an indulgence it was possible to earn a remission of punishment comparable to that earned in the first centuries by Christians who, according to the penitential laws of the early church, made penance for a period of 100 or of 500 days (by fasting, prayer and giving alms).

At the time of the Holy Year 1983-4, Pope John Paul II wrote the following in the bull *Open the Doors to the Redeemer*: 'The Church, the dispenser of grace through the express will of its founder, grants to all the faithful the possibility of access, through the indulgence, to the total gift of God's mercy, but it requires that there be a complete openness and the necessary interior purification, for the indulgence is inseparable from the power of Sacrament of Penance.'

The teaching of indulgences is clearly based on the unbiblical idea that man can and should pay for his punishment himself. In the same bull it says, among other things: 'Sin is ... an offence committed against a just and merciful God, an offence which requires suitable expiation in this life or in the next.'

The new *Code of Canon Law*, promulgated on 25 January 1983 by Pope John Paul II, makes the following points:

'An indulgence is the remission in the sight of God of the temporal punishment due for sins, the guilt of which has already been forgiven. A member of Christ's faithful who is properly disposed and who fulfils certain specific conditions, may gain an indulgence by the help of the Church which, as the minister of redemption, authoritatively dispenses and applies the treasury of the merits of Christ and the Saints.

'An indulgence is partial or plenary according as it partially or wholly frees a person from the temporal punishment due for sins.

'All members of the faithful can gain indulgences, partial or plenary, for themselves, or they can apply them by way of suffrage to the dead.

'Apart from the supreme authority in the Church, only those can grant indulgences to whom this power is either acknowledged in the law, or given by the Roman Pontiff.

'No authority below the Roman Pontiff can give to others the faculty of granting indulgences, unless this authority has been expressly given to the person by the Apostolic See.

'To be capable of gaining indulgences a person must be baptized, not excommunicated, and in the state of grace at least on the completion of the prescribed work.

'To gain them, however, the person who is capable must have at least the intention of gaining them, and must fulfil the prescribed works at the time and in the manner determined by the terms of the grant.

'As far as the granting and the use of indulgences is

concerned, the other provisions contained in the special laws of the Church must also be observed.'⁸

What does the Bible teach?

The Bible knows nothing of any forgiveness of sins by means of indulgences. If the work of salvation accomplished by Christ is perfect, how can any punishment still be required for sin? Peter bears testimony to the fact that Christ bore all our sins on the tree (1 Peter 2:24). That means that he bore in full all the punishment which our sins deserved.

The Bible tells us of the undeserved forgiveness of our sins (Rom. 5:8; Col. 2:13-15; Titus 3:5; Isa. 52:3; Rom. 3:24). We are justified *freely*! So any idea of human achievement is completely done away with.

'I, even I, am he who blots out your transgressions for my own sake; and I will not remember your sins,' says the Lord in Isaiah 43:25. The Lord states clearly in this passage that forgiveness originates with him. It is his work alone, because of his goodness! In Romans 8:3 Paul teaches us that sin was condemned in the flesh when Christ became sin for us.

On this subject Calvin writes, referring to Romans 8:3 and Galatians 3:13, 'The power and curse of sin was destroyed in his flesh when he was offered as a sacrifice, on which the whole weight of our sins was laid, with their curse and execration, with the fearful judgement of God, and condemnation to death.'⁹

No human payment

The Lord does not ask us to settle any accounts.

'Take away all iniquity;
Receive us graciously,
For we will offer the sacrifices of our lips'
(Hosea 14:2).

We have nothing at all to offer to the Lord God which could compensate for our guilt.

No one can by his death help anyone else to expiate his sin:

> 'None of them can by any means redeem his brother,
> Nor give to God a ransom for him'
>
> (Ps. 49:7).

How could 'saints and martyrs' acquire more merit by their death than they needed for themselves? And if they did, how could their surplus of merits be transferred to others? Yet that is what Rome teaches in its statements about the 'treasure of the church'! But the Bible teaches that 'You were not redeemed with corruptible things, like silver or gold, from your aimless conduct received by tradition from your fathers, but with the precious blood of Christ, as of a lamb without blemish and without spot' (1 Peter 1:18-19).

We read in the Bible: 'He who did not spare his own Son, but delivered him up for us all, how shall he not with him also freely give us all things?' (Rom. 8:32). Why do we need to worry and fret any further? Why should we have to do all kinds of things and invent new forms of asceticism so as to 'get back into his good books'? Surely all that we need for salvation is guaranteed to us in Christ?

'Our salvation does not depend on our merits or our zeal, but on the mercy of God,' said Luther.

Augustine said, 'Even if we were to have to die for the sake of another brother, there is not a single drop of martyr's blood which is able to forgive sins: that is the work of Christ. He did it, not so that we should follow his example, but so that we should be thankful to him for it.'[10]

No more punishment for the children of God

The teaching about indulgences is also based on a false understanding of the way in which God chastises his children.

Rome illustrates this by quoting the example of David, who was reproved by the prophet Nathan because of his adultery and murder, and although his sin had been forgiven, he still had to undergo the punishment of losing his son (2 Sam. 12:13-14). Calvin distinguishes between 'judicial punishment' and 'judicial chastisement': 'The one is the act of a judge, the other of a father. When the judge punishes a criminal, he animadverts upon the crime, and demands the penalty. When a father corrects his son sharply, it is not to mulct or avenge, but rather to teach him, and make him more cautious for the future.'[11] That is how God treated David. When he took away David's son from him (2 Sam. 12:18), he corrected him and taught him a lesson.

Paul teaches us the same thing: 'But when we are judged, we are chastened by the Lord, that we may not be condemned with the world' (1 Cor. 11:32).

We read in the epistle to the Hebrews: '"For whom the Lord loves he chastens, and scourges every son whom he receives." If you endure chastening, God deals with you as with sons ... [God chastens us] for our profit, that we may be partakers of his holiness' (Heb. 12:6-10). The Bible does not speak in terms of punishment for sin in the case of the children of God, but it does speak of the discipline of correction.

Augustine even speaks of 'salutary pain'. Chastisement or correction can rightly be called a 'blessing', because it is a proof of God's love, since the Bible tells us in various places,

'Behold, happy is the man whom God corrects;
Therefore do not despise the chastening of the Almighty.
For he bruises, but he binds up;
He wounds, but his hands make whole'
(Job 5:17-18).

'My son, do not despise the chastening of the Lord,
Nor detest his correction;
For whom the Lord loves he corrects,
Just as a father the son in whom he delights'
(Prov. 3:11-12; see also Ps. 94:12).

Calvin teaches, 'The second distinction is, that when the reprobate are brought under the lash of God, they begin in a manner to pay the punishment due to his justice; and though their refusal to listen to these proofs of the divine anger will not escape with impunity, still they are not punished with the view of bringing them to a better mind, but only to teach them by dire experience that God is a judge and avenger. The sons of God are beaten with rods, not that they may pay the punishment due to their faults, but that they may thereby be led to repent. Accordingly, we perceive that they have more respect to the future than to the past. I prefer giving this in the words of Chrysostom rather than my own: "His object in imposing a penalty upon us, is not to inflict punishment on our sins, but to correct us for the future."'[12]

God's forgiveness is complete

Christians who have at some time or other wandered far from the Lord may experience difficulties when trouble strikes them. Is this a punishment which the Lord has sent me because of this sin in my life? Does not the Bible teach plainly that the forgiveness of sins is given by grace without exception?

The tax collector went out of the temple justified. There is no question at all of punishment for his sins (Luke 18:14). Jesus said to the paralysed man, 'Son, be of good cheer; your sins are forgiven you' (Matt. 9:2). Jesus says nothing about penalties as a result of sin which are still to be borne. God's forgiveness is complete.

The Lord says,

'Though your sins are like scarlet,
They shall be as white as snow;
Though they are red like crimson,
They shall be as wool'
(Isa. 1:18; see also Isa. 38:17; 44:22; Micah 7:19; Ps. 32:1).

Augustine teaches on this subject, 'If God has covered sin, it is because he did not want to see it. If he did not want to see it, it is because he did not want to take notice of it. He did not want to punish it; he did not want to know it; he preferred to forget them. Otherwise, why would he have said that sins were to be covered, unless it was so that they should be hidden from his sight? For what else could he do if he saw them, but punish them?'

Grace alone

It would be foolish to say that the trials of life were sent to us by God in order to punish us for sin. On the other hand, we need to realize that conflict and suffering are good and useful. We learn through them not to seek in ourselves what only God can and will give to us. Through the difficulties, we learn to see God's goodness towards us. The difficulties and failures are a themselves a grace of God, for they cause us not only to commit the different aspects of our life to the Lord, but also to consecrate the whole of our lives to him.

I believe also that this 'grace' must underlie every true presentation of the gospel. Consequently, a life which seeks salvation in merits is miserable and empty. This trade in indulgences is a gigantic religious hoax!

'[Indulgences], to describe them truly, are a profanation of the blood of Christ, and a delusion of Satan, by which the Christian people are led away from the grace of God and the life which is in Christ, and turned aside from the true way of salvation. For how could the blood of Christ be more shamefully profaned than by denying its sufficiency for the remission of sins, for reconciliation and satisfaction, unless its defects, as if it were dried up and exhausted, are supplemented from some other quarter? Peter's words are: "To him give all the prophets witness, that through his name whosoever believeth in him shall receive remission of sins" (Acts 10:43); but indulgences bestow the remission of sins through Peter, Paul, and the martyrs. "The blood of Jesus Christ his Son cleanseth us from all sin," says John (1 John

1:7). Indulgences make the blood of the martyrs an ablution of sins. "He hath made him to be sin (i.e. a satisfaction for sin) for us who knew no sin," says Paul (2 Cor. 5:21), "that we might be made the righteousness of God in him." Indulgences make the satisfaction of sin to depend on the blood of the martyrs. Paul exclaimed and testified to the Corinthians, that Christ alone was crucified, and died for them (1 Cor. 1:13). Indulgences declare that Paul and others died for us. Paul elsewhere says that Christ purchased the church with his own blood (Acts 20:28). Indulgences assign another purchase to the blood of martyrs. "By one offering he hath perfected for ever them that are sanctified," says the apostle (Heb. 10:14). Indulgences, on the other hand, insist that sanctification, which would otherwise be insufficient, is perfected by martyrs. John says that all the saints "have washed their robes, and made them white in the blood of the Lamb" (Rev. 7:14). Indulgences tell us to wash our robes in the blood of saints.'[13]

In his *Explanation of the statements about indulgences*, Luther sums up in a few words the message of the gospel — the very holy gospel of the glory of the grace of God: 'It is from this gospel that the true glory of God is born, when we learn that it is not by our works, but by the grace of the merciful God; that the law is fulfilled in Christ, not by works but by faith, not because of a human sacrifice to God, but in receiving everything from Christ and in our being thus united to him.' May we also have this firm assurance that the real treasure of the church is in fact this holy gospel of the glory and the grace of God!

I cannot close this chapter on indulgences without referring to a warning issued by Calvin: 'Undoubtedly either the gospel of God or indulgences must be false. That Christ is offered to us in the gospel with all the abundance of heavenly blessings, with all his merits, all his righteousness, wisdom, and grace, without exception, Paul bears witness when he says, "Now then we are ambassadors for Christ, as though God did beseech you by us: we pray you in Christ's stead, be ye reconciled to God. For he hath made him to be sin for us, who knew no sin; that we might be made the righteousness of God in him" (2 Cor. 5:20-21). And what is meant by the fellowship of Christ, which, according to the same apostle (1 Cor. 1:9), is offered to us in the gospel, all believers know. On the contrary, indulgences, bringing forth some portion of the grace of God from the armoury of the pope, fix it to lead, parchment, and a particular place, but dissever it from the Word of God.'[14]

5.
Luther's Ninety-Five Theses[1]

Out of love and zeal for truth and the desire to bring it to light, the following theses will be publicly discussed at Wittenberg under the chairmanship of the reverend father Martin Luther, Master of Arts and Sacred Theology and regularly appointed lecturer on these subjects at that place. He requests that those who cannot be present to debate orally with us will do so by letter.

In the name of our Lord Jesus Christ. Amen.

1. When our Lord and Master Jesus Christ said, 'Repent', he willed the entire life of believers to be one of repentance.

2. This word cannot be understood as referring to the sacrament of penance, that is, confession and satisfaction, as administered by the clergy.

3. Yet it does not mean solely inner repentance; such inner repentance is worthless unless it produces various outward mortifications of the flesh.

4. The penalty of sin remains as long as the hatred of self, that is, true inner repentance, until our entrance into the kingdom of heaven.

5. The pope neither desires nor is able to remit any penalties except those imposed by his own authority or that of the canons.

6. The pope cannot remit any guilt, except by declaring and showing that it has been remitted by God; or, to be sure, by remitting guilt in cases reserved to his judgement. If his right to grant remission in these cases were disregarded, the guilt would certainly remain unforgiven.

7. God remits guilt to no one unless at the same time he humbles him in all things and makes him submissive to his vicar, the priest.

8. The penitential canons are imposed only on the living, and, according to the canons themselves, nothing should be imposed on the dying.

9. Therefore the Holy Spirit through the pope is kind to us insofar as the pope in his decrees always makes exception of the article of death and of necessity.

10. Those priests act ignorantly and wickedly who, in the case of the dying, reserve canonical penalties for purgatory.

11. Those tares of changing the canonical penalty to the penalty of purgatory were evidently sown while the bishops slept.

12. In former times canonical penalties were imposed, not after, but before absolution, as tests of true contrition.

13. The dying are freed by death from all penalties, are already dead as far as the canon laws are concerned, and have a right to be released from them.

14. Imperfect piety or love on the part of the dying person necessarily brings with it great fear; and the smaller the love, the greater the fear.

15. This fear or horror is sufficient in itself, to say nothing of other things, to constitute the penalty of purgatory, since it is very near the horror of despair.

16. Hell, purgatory and heaven seem to differ the same as despair, fear and assurance of salvation.

17. It seems as though for the souls in purgatory fear should necessarily decrease and love increase.

18. Furthermore, it does not seem proved, either by reason or Scripture, that souls in purgatory are outside the state of merit, that is, unable to grow in love.

19. Nor does it seem proved that souls in purgatory, at least not all of them, are certain and assured of their own salvation, even if we ourselves may be entirely certain of it.

20. Therefore the pope, when he uses the words 'plenary remission of all penalties', does not actually mean 'all penalties', but only those imposed by himself.

21. Thus those indulgence preachers are in error who say that a man is absolved from every penalty and saved by papal indulgences.

22. As a matter of fact, the pope remits to souls in purgatory no penalty which, according to canon law, they should have paid in this life.

23. If remission of all penalties whatsoever could be granted to anyone at all, certainly it would be granted only to the most perfect, that is, to very few.

24. For this reason most people are necessarily deceived by that indiscriminate and high-sounding promise of release from penalty.

25. That power which the pope has in general over purgatory corresponds to the power which any bishop or curate has in a particular way in his own diocese or parish.

26. The pope does very well when he grants remission to souls in purgatory, not by the power of the keys, which he does not have, but by way of intercession for them.

27. They preach only human doctrines who say that as soon as the money clinks into the money chest, the soul flies out of purgatory.

28. It is certain that when money clinks in the money chest, greed and avarice can be increased; but when the church intercedes, the result is in the hands of God alone.

29. Who knows whether all souls in purgatory wish to be redeemed, since we have exceptions in St Severinus and St Paschal, as related in a legend.

30. No one is sure of the integrity of his own contrition, much less of having received plenary remission.

31. The man who actually buys indulgences is as rare as he who is really penitent; indeed, he is exceedingly rare.

32. Those who believe that they can be certain of their salvation because they have indulgence letters will be eternally damned, together with their teachers.

33. Men must especially be on their guard against those who say that the pope's pardons are that inestimable gift of God by which man is reconciled to him.

34. For the graces of indulgences are concerned only with the penalties of sacramental satisfaction established by man.

35. They who teach that contrition is not necessary on the part of those who intend to buy souls out of purgatory or to buy confessional privileges preach unchristian doctrine.

36. Any truly repentant Christian has a right to full remission of penalty and guilt, even without indulgence letters.

37. Any true Christian, whether living or dead, participates in all the blessings of Christ and the church; and this is granted him by God, even without indulgence letters.

38. Nevertheless, papal remission and blessing are by no means to be disregarded, for they are, as I have said, the proclamation of the divine remission.

39. It is very difficult, even for the most learned theologians, at one and the same time to commend to the people the bounty of indulgences and the need of true contrition.

40. A Christian who is truly contrite seeks and loves to pay penalties for his sins; the bounty of indulgences, however, relaxes penalties and causes men to hate them — at least it furnishes occasion for hating them.

41. Papal indulgences must be preached with caution, lest people erroneously think that they are preferable to other good works of love.

42. Christians are to be taught that the pope does not intend that the buying of indulgences should in any way be compared with works of mercy.

43. Christians are to be taught that he who gives to the poor or lends to the needy does a better deed than he who buys indulgences.

44. Because love grows by works of love, man thereby becomes better. Man does not, however, become better by means of indulgences but is merely freed from penalties.

45. Christians are to be taught that he who sees a needy man and passes him by, yet gives his money for indulgences, does not buy papal indulgences but God's wrath.

46. Christians are to be taught that, unless they have more than they need, they must reserve enough for their family needs and by no means squander it on indulgences.

47. Christians are to be taught that the buying of indulgences is a matter of free choice, not commanded.

48. Christians are to be taught that the pope, in granting

indulgences, needs and thus desires their devout prayer more than their money.

49. Christians are to be taught that papal indulgences are useful only if they do not put their trust in them, but very harmful if they lose their fear of God because of them.

50. Christians are to be taught that if the pope knew the exactions of the indulgence preachers, he would rather that the basilica of St Peter were burned to ashes than built up with the skin, flesh and bones of his sheep.

51. Christians are to be taught that the pope would and should wish to give of his own money, even though he had to sell the basilica of St Peter, to many of those from whom certain hawkers of indulgences cajole money.

52. It is vain to trust in salvation by indulgence letters, even though the indulgence commissary, or even the pope, were to offer his soul as security.

53. They are enemies of Christ and the pope who forbid altogether the preaching of the Word of God in some churches in order that indulgences may be preached in others.

54. Injury is done the Word of God when, in the same sermon, an equal or larger amount of time is devoted to indulgences than to the Word.

55. It is certainly the pope's sentiment that if indulgences, which are a very insignificant thing, are celebrated with one bell, one procession and one ceremony, then the gospel, which is the very greatest thing, should be preached with a hundred bells, a hundred processions, a hundred ceremonies.

56. The treasures of the church, out of which the pope distributes indulgences, are not sufficiently discussed or known among the people of Christ.

57. That indulgences are not temporal treasures is certainly clear, for many indulgence sellers do not distribute them freely but only gather them.

58. Nor are they the merits of Christ and the saints, for, even without the pope, the latter always work grace for the inner man, and the cross, death and hell for the outer man.

59.   St. Laurence said that the poor of the church were the treasures of the church, but he spoke according to the usage of the word in his own time.

60.   Without want of consideration we say that the keys of the church, given by the merits of Christ, are that treasure;

61.   For it is clear that the pope's power is of itself sufficient for the remission of penalties and cases reserved by himself.

62.   The true treasure of the church is the most holy gospel of the glory and grace of God.

63.   But this treasure is naturally most odious, for it makes the first to be last.

64.   On the other hand, the treasure of indulgences is naturally most acceptable, for it makes the last to be first.

65.   Therefore the treasures of the gospel are nets with which one formerly fished for men of wealth.

66.   The treasures of indulgences are nets with which one now fishes for the wealth of men.

67.   The indulgences which the demagogues acclaim as the greatest graces are actually understood to be such only insofar as they promote gain.

68.   They are nevertheless in truth the most insignificant graces when compared with the grace of God and the piety of the cross.

69.   Bishops and curates are bound to admit the commissaries of papal indulgences with all reverence.

70.   But they are much more bound to strain their eyes and ears lest these men preach their own dreams instead of what the pope has commissioned.

71.   Let him who speaks against the truth concerning papal indulgences be anathema and accursed;

72.   But let him who guards against the lust and licence of the indulgence preachers be blessed;

73.   Just as the pope justly thunders against those who by any means whatsoever contrive harm to the sale of indulgences.

74.   But much more does he intend to thunder against those who use indulgences as a pretext to contrive harm to holy love and truth.

75. To consider papal indulgences so great that they could absolve a man even if he had done the impossible and had violated the mother of God is madness.

76. We say on the contrary that papal indulgences cannot remove the very least of venial sins as far as guilt is concerned.

77. To say that even St Peter, if he were now pope, could not grant greater graces is blasphemy against St Peter and the pope.

78. We say on the contrary that even the present pope, or any pope whatsoever, has greater graces at his disposal, that is, the gospel, spiritual powers, gifts of healing, etc., as it is written in 1 Corinthins 12.

79. To say that the cross emblazoned with the papal coat of arms, and set up by the indulgence preachers, is equal in worth to the cross of Christ is blasphemy.

80. The bishops, curates and theologians who permit such talk to be spread among the people will have to answer for this.

81. This unbridled preaching of indulgences makes it difficult even for learned men to rescue the reverence which is due the pope from slander or from the shrewd questions of the laity,

82. Such as: 'Why does not the pope empty purgatory for the sake of holy love and the dire need of the souls that are there if he redeems an infinite number of souls for the sake of miserable money with which to build a church? The former reasons would be most just; the latter is most trivial.'

83. Again, 'Why are funeral and anniversary masses for the dead continued and why does he not return or permit the withdrawal of the endowments founded for them, since it is wrong to pray for the redeemed?'

84. Again, 'What is this new piety of God and the pope that for a consideration of money they permit a man who is impious and their enemy to buy out of purgatory the pious soul of a friend of God and do not rather, because of the need of that pious and beloved soul, free it for pure love's sake?'

85. Again, 'Why are the penitential canons, long since

abrogated and dead in actual fact and through disuse, now satisfied by the granting of indulgences as though they were still alive and in force?'

86.   Again, 'Why does not the pope, whose wealth is today greater than the wealth of the richest Crassus, build this one basilica of St Peter with his own money rather than with the money of poor believers?'

87.   Again, 'What does the pope remit or grant to those who by perfect contrition already have a right to full remission and blessings?'

88.   Again, 'What greater blessings could come to the church than if the pope were to bestow these remissions and blessings on every believer a hundred times a day, as he now does but once?'

89.   'Since the pope seeks the salvation of souls rather than money by his indulgences, why does he suspend the indulgences and pardons previously granted when they have equal efficacy?'

90.   To repress these very sharp arguments of the laity by force alone, and not to resolve them by giving reasons, is to expose the church and the pope to the ridicule of their enemies and to make Christians unhappy.

91.   If, therefore, indulgences were preached according to the spirit and intention of the pope, all these doubts would be readily resolved. Indeed, they would not exist.

92.   Away then with all those prophets who say to the people of Christ, 'Peace, peace,' and there is no peace!

93.   Blessed be all those prophets who say to the people of Christ, 'Cross, cross,' and there is no cross!

94.   Christians should be exhorted to be diligent in following Christ, their head, through penalties, death and hell;

95.   And thus be confident of entering into heaven through many tribulations rather than through the false security of peace (Acts 14:22).

In these ninety-five theses, Luther accuses those who sold indulgences, and in particular the well-known Dominican monk, Tetzel, of preaching a false gospel! It is a gospel which man has invented, saying that man can be reconciled with God by means of indulgences (33) and that he can be saved by the purchase of an indulgence (21).

Luther reproves them for recommending indulgences as being the 'greatest gifts of grace' (67). The preaching on indulgences had cast a shadow on the preaching of the Word of God (53, 54).

We can see for ourselves the exasperation which Luther felt when faced with the greed for money displayed by the sellers of indulgences (65-67). He is vehement in his attacks not only on the preachers themselves, but also on those who flock to hear them preach (24, 32). Eternal damnation awaits them. Although at first he did not totally reject the concept of indulgences, Luther teaches that these cannot make any contribution to salvation (52, 76, 33). He also says that an indulgence has no power to change the heart of man for the better.

Luther restores the preaching of the gospel to its place as the true treasure of the church (62). Charitable works performed without any thought of self-interest and acts of mercy are of much greater worth than the money spent on the purchase of an indulgence (41-43). In these theses, he denies any power that the pope or the church may claim to exercise over the dead (13).

In 1517 Luther had not yet completely broken with the whole idea of purgatory, as we can see in reading these theses. The Roman Catholic Church believed — and still believes — that souls must be cleansed by bearing the punishment of their sins in purgatory. These penances were respectively: penalties imposed by the church, and which were regarded as coming from God; and those which priests could impose on sinners. Luther rescued the souls in purgatory from the hands of the priests and committed them to the mercy of God. He rejected the practice of the Roman Catholic Church which forced men, and, even worse, ordered the dying, to do penance even in purgatory (10). Luther declared that the dead are freed from the power of the church. The church can no longer require anything of them. So purgatory is left to collapse, like a house of cards!

This practice of indulgences is a huge waste of time! It is not by indulgences, but by the preaching of the gospel that man can have access to the spiritual riches available in Jesus Christ (37).

Those who preach about indulgences and the sufferings of purgatory are false prophets. When we read a sermon which Luther preached in 1517, we can see the radical and shocking way in which he treated this subject. I leave the reader to be the judge of what he felt! The glory of God and the salvation of man are at stake: 'Indulgences have nothing to do with true godliness. The man who buys indulgences does not only want to be free from the punishments which he deserves; he is more concerned about the punishment than about the sin itself. So indulgences encourage pride, and selfish desires to protect oneself. They encourage a false confidence and leave the door wide open for sin... We need to come to Christ, but, alas, that is not what is preached. The preaching is all about indulgences. We live in very sad times, even darker than in Egypt of old. The priests are snoring and everyone is fast asleep!'

It seems to me that these ninety-five theses of Luther's are still relevant today.

6.
The communion of saints

In an attempt to give biblical support to its teaching about indulgences, Rome often quotes Colossians 1:24: 'I now rejoice in my sufferings for you, and fill up in my flesh what is lacking in the afflictions of Christ, for the sake of his body, which is the church.'

This verse is misused by those who want to hold to their own personal idea of what the church is. The teaching about indulgences has its roots in the unbiblical concept of the 'communion of the saints'.

According to Rome, the church is not limited to the communion which is visible here below, on earth, but also includes the souls in purgatory as well as those of the saints in heaven. Between all these souls there exists a community of life and of possessions, known as the 'communion of the saints'. There is a spiritual union between the church militant (the believers on earth), the suffering church (the souls in purgatory) and the glorified church (the saints in heaven). Since they are all members of one body, they also have spiritual possessions in common. So, for example, souls in purgatory are helped by the prayers, good works and indulgences of believers on earth, and especially by the sacrifice of the mass.

The common denominator in this concept of the communion of saints is the idea of merit. So, according to Rome, the various works performed by the living for the benefit of the souls in purgatory have a twofold redemptive function, by discharge of debts and by prayer.

As to the discharge or payment of debts, the blessings of Christ and of the saints are applied to the suffering soul by means of the mass and of indulgences. The good works of believers also count in this aspect of the discharge of debts. Almost all good works are difficult to perform and so carry with them the power to discharge temporal penalties, not only for the person who performs the work, but also for others who are in a state of grace. So by prayer, fasting, almsgiving, etc., we can pay the debts of suffering brothers and sisters.

Prayers, on the other hand, have an influence on God's decisions, according to Christ's promise: 'Ask, and you will receive' (John 16:24). The merits of Christ and of the saints can be applied to the souls of those who suffer. We should note that the prayers and good works done on behalf of believing souls are not on that account of no value for ourselves; on the contrary, their value is even greater, because they are offered in a spirit of pure love.[1]

After the Second Vatican Council, the idea of solidarity with those who are suffering once again became important in the Catholic understanding of the communion of saints. Pope John Paul II, in his address to the cardinals and members of the Curia, made the following statement: 'Salvation opens to us the pages of a wonderful book speaking of solidarity with a suffering Christ and, in him, leads us to the heart of the mystery of our solidarity with our suffering brethren. The jubilee of salvation will make possible a more intense life by the Spirit in the communion of saints. Suffering is the lot of every human being. Everyone has his part to play in salvation, and even when this has been brought to complete fulfilment, there will still be the need for this great mystery, the offering up of a very heavy burden representing the sufferings and sicknesses of mankind. So, "In my body, I make up what is lacking of the afflictions of Christ, for the sake of his body, which is the church."'

The Roman Catholic concept of the 'communion of saints' is a false doctrine, which dishonours the person of Christ and which we must reject totally. This teaching is radically opposed to the gospel of grace!

Communion by the Holy Spirit

The biblical teaching on the communion of saints does not include any idea of merit. According to the Bible, the communion of saints includes the saints who are under grace, with a view to the work of service (Eph. 4:12; 1 Peter 2:9). It is a communion of those who persevere in the teaching of the apostles, in fellowship with the brethren, in breaking of bread and in prayers (Acts 2:42). It is the communion of those who watch over each other, among whom none is destitute, and there is none who regards his possessions as his alone (Acts 4:32). It is a communion where the differences which cause divisions in society have disappeared (Gal. 3:26-28). The communion of saints is a fellowship by the Holy Spirit, which has been given in the church and which unites the believers in Christ (Rom. 8:9).

The basis of the communion of saints is union with Christ. In him they form one body and serve each other in love. This biblical concept of the communion of saints is clearly set out in the *Heidelberg Catechism*: 'What do you understand by the communion of saints? First, that believers, all and every one, as members of Christ, are partakers of him and of all his treasures and gifts; second, that every one must know himself bound to employ his gifts readily and cheerfully for the advantage and salvation of other members (1 John 1:3: Rom. 8:32: 1 Cor. 12:12-13; 6:17; 12:21; 13:1,5; Phil. 2:4-8).'[2]

What great comfort the Word of God offers to us by assuring us that we are saved by grace, by faith! How sad for the Roman Catholic believer to have to live with the thought that the suffering and pain of one human being can contribute to the salvation of another!

We should understand Colossians 1:24 in terms of suffering for righteousness' sake. Paul is not talking about the suffering of mankind in general, which is the lot of both Christians and non-Christians, but about suffering for righteousness' sake. He is thinking of suffering for the cause of Christ. It is clear that this suffering does not reconcile us

to God. That is the work of the Lord Jesus alone. Paul has
nothing to add to that, for the work of reconciliation
accomplished by Jesus is perfect!

But in Colossians 1:24 he is talking about the suffering
which Jesus endured as a witness for God. Jesus came to
warn his fellow men that they were wallowing in sin and that
their only hope was in the grace of God. He told them plainly
that he was to suffer and die on the cross. That was why he
suffered as a man. He suffered because of righteousness.
Paul, who followed in Christ's steps, also knew what it was
to suffer in this way (2 Cor. 6:4-10). He did his share in filling
up the part of this suffering which was still lacking. That
means that Jesus had not revealed all the purposes of God.
We read in John 16:12 that he still had many things to say to
his disciples and that he could not do so yet because they
were not yet able to bear these things. It was only with the
coming of the Spirit of truth that the Holy Spirit, speaking
through Paul, would reveal the whole counsel of God. Paul
'fulfilled the Word'. Paul revealed the mystery of the
church, and since the time of Paul there is no other truth
about God which is still to be revealed. These extraordinary
revelations of the counsels of God through the agency of
Paul were accompanied by much suffering and pain. So Paul
could rightly say that he had filled up what was lacking of the
sufferings of Christ. That, I believe, is the meaning of
Colossians 1:24.

This has nothing at all to do with the Catholic teaching
about the communion of saints. As Calvin put it, 'Far be it
from us to imagine that Paul thought anything was wanting
to the sufferings of Christ in regard to the complete fulness
of righteousness, salvation, and life, or that he wished to
make any addition to it, after showing so clearly and
eloquently that the grace of Christ was poured out in such
rich abundance as far to exceed all the power of sin (Rom.
5:15). All saints have been saved by it alone, not by the merit
of their own life or death, as Peter distinctly testifies (Acts
15:11); so that it is an insult to God and his Anointed to place
the worthiness of any saint in anything save the mercy of

God alone. But why dwell longer on this, as if the matter were obscure, when to mention these monstrous dogmas is to refute them?'[3]

7.
Conclusion:
the message of the gospel

The Lord God is holy. He is good and true. His eyes are too pure to look on evil; therefore he hates all forms of lying, trickery and deceit. Lying lips are an abomination to him (Prov. 12:22). Paul tells us in Ephesians 4 to put away lying.

God wants us to know the truth about ourselves, but this truth confounds and humbles us: 'Let God be true but every man a liar' (Rom. 3:4). We are children of wrath, says the Bible. We are all, without exception, under sin:

'As it is written:

"There is none righteous, no, not one;
There is none who understands;
There is none who seeks after God.
They have all gone out of the way;
They have together become unprofitable;
There is none who does good, no, not one,"
"Their throat is an open tomb;
With their tongues they have practised deceit";
"The poison of asps is under their lips";
"Whose mouth is full of cursing and bitterness."
"Their feet are swift to shed blood;
Destruction and misery are in their ways;
And the way of peace they have not known."
"There is no fear of God before their eyes"'
(Rom. 3:10-18; see also v.9).

That is a description of man — incapable of doing anything at all that is good and always inclined to evil. That

is what man is like. He 'drinks iniquity like water' (Job
15:16). That is the truth, the divine testimony about man. It
is not a flattering description — on the contrary. We can only
blush with shame, cover our faces and dissolve in grief when
we see our own misery in the light of his majesty.

However, we are so full of ourselves, our own merits and
abilities! We always want to be seen in the best possible light
and if we do happen to do some good deed, even this is spoilt
by our pride and our terrible urge to show off. How could we
ever free ourselves from our own evil nature? We were all
born in iniquity, conceived in sin. Are we ready to
acknowledge that before God — not only to confess our evil
deeds, thoughts and words, but also to acknowledge that we
ourselves are sinners before God and to admit that the whole
of our lives are marred by sin?

That alone is the way of salvation. Only in this way can
we share in the gospel of grace. The gospel tells us that, from
the beginning, God saw the awful misery into which we all,
beginning with our ancestors Adam and Eve, had fallen
because of our sins. He could have judged us once and for all
and condemned us, for his justice demands payment in time
and in eternity, in our souls as well as our bodies, for the sins
committed against his holy majesty.

We could never escape this punishment without God's
justice being satisfied. God will by no means clear the guilty
(Exod. 34:7).

Sin must be punished; the wages of sin must be paid;
justice must take its course. But — wonder of wonders! —
God himself, by his Son, paid the price himself. We hear him
utter words of love and mercy which until then were
unknown: 'God is love' (1 John 4:16). 'For God so loved the
world that he gave his only begotten Son, that whoever
believes in him should not perish but have everlasting life'
(John 3:16).

God does not look for anything at all of value in us. He
does not ask us to thank him by good actions; we are quite
simply incapable of performing any. 'Since, therefore, we
are unable to make that satisfaction in our own persons, or to

deliver ourselves from the wrath of God, he has been pleased of his infinite mercy to give his only begotten Son for our Surety, who was made sin, and became a curse for us and in our stead, that he might make satisfaction to divine justice on our behalf.'[1] He, the Son of God, became man and, as the Lamb of God, took on himself all our sins (John 1:29).

We cannot pay for ourselves; we cannot deliver ourselves from the wrath of God. God made him to be sin for us. He was rejected as someone who is accursed: 'Christ has redeemed us from the curse of the law, having become a curse for us (for it is written, "Cursed is everyone who hangs on a tree")' (Gal. 3:13). He died in our place, our one and only true Saviour. We can therefore rest on his perfect and completed work.

By raising his Son from the dead, the Father showed us that the debt had been paid, for Christ 'was delivered up because of our offences, and was raised because of our justification' (Rom. 4:25).

God only asks us to believe, to believe in his love, to believe in Jesus Christ, in his perfect work of salvation. The promise of the gospel is now that all who believe in the crucified Christ will not perish, but have eternal life. 'He who believes in me has everlasting life,' said Jesus Christ (John 6:47). Those who truly believe receive this blessing and that is pure grace — the grace of God!

That is the wonderful promise of the gospel of free grace. My desire and prayer is that you also may share in this glory by grace. On this subject Peter writes, 'You greatly rejoice ... that the genuineness of your faith, being much more precious than gold that perishes, though it is tested by fire, may be found to praise, honour, and glory at the revelation of Jesus Christ, whom having not seen you love. Though now you do not see him, yet believing, you rejoice with joy inexpressible and full of glory, receiving the end of your faith — the salvation of your souls' (1 Peter 1:7-9).

References

Introduction
1. Translated from Luther's *Autobiographical Fragment* (March 1545).

Chapter 1
1. *Council of Orange*, 7, 180.
2. *Canons and Decrees of the Council of Trent,* (trans. T. A. Buckley), George Routledge & Co., Session VI, ch. XVI, canons 2-3.
3. *Council of Orange,* dec. 200.
4. *Council of Trent,* VI, XVI, 5.
5. *Council of Trent,* V, dec. 1.
6. F. v. d. Meer, *Catechism,* 82-83.
7. Translated from B. Meyer, *Catholic Apologetics,* 1946.
8. Blaise Pascal, *Pensées,* (ed. Lafuma) J. Delmas & Cie 1960, 830.
9. John Calvin, *Institutes of the Christian Religion,* trans. H. Beveridge, Eerdmans, II, III, 6.
10. *Ibid.,* II, II, 7.
11. *Canons of Dort,* III-IV, 16.

Chapter 2
1. *Heidelberg Catechism,* XLIV, 115.
2. *Ibid.,* II, 3.
3. Calvin, *Institutes,* II, XVI, 3.
4. *Ibid.,* II, XVI, 5.
5. *Ibid.,* II, XVI, 6.

6. *Ibid.,* II, XVI, 6.
7. *Malines Catechism,* question 153.
8. *Catholic Catechism for Adults,* p.244.
9. *Council of Trent,* VI, IV.
10. *Ibid.,* VI, V.
11. K. H. Miskotte, *Exposition of the Heidelberg Catechism.*
12. *Council of Trent,* VI, XVI, 9.
13. *Catholic Catechism for Adults,* p.237.
14. *Council of Trent,* VI, VII.
15. *Ibid.,* VI, VII.
16. Calvin, *Institutes,* III, XI, 2.
17. *Ibid.,* III, XI, 3.
18. See Berkouwer's dogmatic study, *Faith and Justification.*
19. *Canons of Dort,* 1 - X
20. Calvin, *Institutes,* III, XI, 5.
21. *Council of Trent,* VI, II.
22. Calvin, *Institutes,* III, XI, 6.
23. *Ibid.,* III, XI, 5.
24. H. Bavinck, *Reformed Dogmatics,* IV, 233.
25. Calvin, *Institutes,* III, VII, 1.

Chapter 3
1. *Council of Trent,* VI, XVI, 1.
2. *Ibid.,* VI, XVI, 20.
3. *Ibid.,* VI, XVI, 32.
4. *Potters' Catechism*
5. *Council of Trent,* VI, XVI.
6. Calvin, *Institutes,* III, XVIII, 2.
7. *Ibid.,* III, XVIII, 3.
8. *Ibid.,* III, XVIII, 7.
9. *Ibid.,* III, XV, 1, 2, 3.
10. *Ibid.,* III, XV, 5.
11. Calvin, *The Necessity of Reforming the Church, Calvin's Tracts,* Eerdmans, 1958, vol. 1, pp.193-4.

Chapter 4
1. Translated from Cardinal de Jong, *Manual of Church History,* pp. 536-7.
2. Luther, *Exhortation to all Clergy Assembled at Augsburg, Luther's Works,* Muhlenberg Press, vol. 34, pp. 14-15.
3. Luther himself was later to say of his views at this period, 'My

main concern, however, is to beg my pious reader ... to read my books judiciously — or rather with much mercy. He should realize that I was once a monk, and that when I first took up this cause I was a most vehement papist... This is why you will find in my earlier writings such a multitude of grovelling concessions to the pope, which as time has proceeded I abominate and repudiate for extreme blasphemy. You will, then, pious reader, lay this error, or as my critics falsely describe it, this self-contradiction — to the charge of the time and my inexperience' (Luther's *Autobiographical Fragment,* quoted in E. G. Rupp & B. Drewery (eds), *Martin Luther,* Edward Arnold, 1970, pp.173-4).(Translator's note.)

4. *New Catholic Catechism for Adults,* p.370.
5. *Council of Trent,* XIV, VIII.
6. Paul VI, *Apostolic Constitution Promulgating the Revision of Sacred Indulgences,* Catholic Truth Society, p.20.
7. *Ibid.,* p.9.
8. *Code of Canon Law,* Collins, 1984, p. 178, Canons 992-7.
9. Calvin, *Institutes,* III, IV, 27.
10. Augustine, *Tract on John,* 84.
11. Calvin, *Institutes,* III, IV, 31.
12. *Ibid.,* III, IV, 33.
13. *Ibid.,* III, V, 2.
14. *Ibid.,* III, V, 5.

Chapter 5
1. The text of the Ninety-Five Theses is reproduced from *Luther's Ninety-Five Theses,* trans. C. M. Jacobs, rev. H. J. Grimm, Fortress Press, 1957.

Chapter 6
1. Mgr Potters, *Explanation of the Catechism,* III.
2. *Heidelberg Catechism,* XXI, 55.
3. Calvin, *Institutes,* III, V, 4.

Conclusion
1. *Canons of Dort,* II, 2.